The Th

of Stratford-upon-Avon

1875 - 1992

An Architectural History

by

Marian J. Pringle

Stratford-upon-Avon

1994

The Theatres of Stratford-upon-Avon, by Marian J. Pringle
(Stratford-upon-Avon Papers No. 5)

Published by the Stratford-upon-Avon Society, with financial support from the Royal Shakespeare Theatre and the Shakespeare Birthplace Trust.

ISBN 0951 417 819

Other titles in this series are:

1. *The Town Hall, Stratford-upon-Avon,*
   by Mairi Macdonald, 1986.

2. *The Shrieve's House, Stratford-upon-Avon,*
   by Peta Rée, 1987.

3. *Lord Ronald Gower's Monument to Shakespeare,*
   by Michael Kimberley, 1989.

4. *The Market House, Stratford-upon-Avon,*
   by Robert Bearman, 1990.

Printed in Great Britain by
Ebenezer Baylis and Son Ltd,
The Trinity Press, Worcester, and London

The Theatres of Stratford-upon-Avon 1875-1992

An Architectural History

The Shakespeare Memorial Theatre, from the south, 1889.

The Royal Shakespeare Theatre, river view looking south, 1992.

Contents

ILLUSTRATIONS

9. Fountain court and staircase:
    a. 1932.
    b. 1971.

10. Auditorium, view towards the stage:
    a. 1932.
    b. 1962.
    c. 1993.

11. Auditorium, view from the stage:
    a. 1932.
    b. 1974.

12. Shakespeare Memorial Theatre, from the north, 1947.
    Inset: Kennington sculpture 'Treachery'.

13. Some details surviving in 1993:
    a&b. Gargoyles (1880).
    c. Hermes door handle (1932).
    d. Stonework and Kummer terra-cotta panels (1880s).
    e. Woodwork on restaurant entrance door (1932).

14. a. Memorial Theatre from the river, c.1900.
    b. Swan Theatre from the gardens, 1993.

15. a. Conference Hall, c.1950.
    b. Swan Theatre, interior, 1986.

16. a. The Studio, interior, 1965.
    b. The Other Place, exterior, 1992.

Plans:

1. Shakespeare Memorial Theatre, 1879.
2. 1932 Ground plan, showing surviving parts of the first theatre.
3. a. East elevation to river, 1932.
    b. West elevation, 1932.
4. Cross sections 1932:
    a. through auditorium.
    b. through stage.
5. 1932/1976 comparative section and plan (Iain Mackintosh).
6. Swan Theatre ground plan, 1985 (Michael Reardon & Associates).
7. The Other Place, 1991 (Michael Reardon & Associates).

Acknowledgements

I have much enjoyed writing this book which has given me the chance for further exploration of two of my foremost interests: the less frequented regions of Shakespeare stage history, and architectural history.

I am grateful to the Stratford-upon-Avon Society's Chairman, Dr. Robert Bearman, for the suggestion that I write this history of one of Stratford's two world-famous buildings (the other, of course, being Shakespeare's Birthplace) and for his advice throughout the project. Among those whose help has been much appreciated are David Brierley, Ann Daniels, Dennis Flower, Lady Flower, Brian Glover, Jonathan Pope, Graham Sawyer and architects Bob Harvey and Michael Reardon. I owe thanks also for the support, assistance and patience of my colleagues, Mairi Macdonald, Sylvia Morris and Mary White as I traced and found obscure details, and to Malcolm Davies for his careful attention in preparing the photographs for illustrations. Sue Rudd has provided helpful design advice.

Particular appreciation must be recorded to Sir Geoffrey Jellicoe and to Dame Elizabeth Chesterton who helped to resolve questions about the relationship between the architects of the 1932 theatre. Without the financial backing of the Royal Shakespeare Theatre and the Shakespeare Birthplace Trust the work could not have been published.

The greatest debt, for support, interest and encouragement at all times is to Roger to whom the work is dedicated.

Marian J. Pringle
September 1993

Prologue

Stratford-upon-Avon was already a centre for tourist pilgrimage by the eighteenth century. The Garrick Jubilee of 1769, the Shakespeare Tercentenary of 1864 and the subsequent foundation, in 1875, of the Shakespeare Memorial Theatre have followed on from the early travellers' visits so that today over a million people each year come to this essentially small English market town to see where the poet and dramatist William Shakespeare lived and died, and to pay tribute to his work in the theatres built in his memory.

A variety of good and reliable histories of the Shakespeare Memorial Theatre and its theatrical work have been written, notably by T. C. Kemp and J. C. Trewin, and by Sally Beauman.[1] This present work makes no attempt to look at the achievements of the actors and directors of Stratford's stages but is intended as a record of some aspects of the buildings in which they worked; for the Shakespeare Memorial Theatre and now the Royal Shakespeare Theatre, the Swan, and The Other Place are testaments in their own right to other kinds of artistic excellence.

The talents of architects, builders and craftsmen are all too often ignored by the audiences who come for the more immediate enjoyment of plays at Stratford, and who depart without even a cursory glance at the walls of the crowded interval bars or the sparkling water in the foyer fountain. The theatres' surroundings are necessarily secondary to the work that goes on within them; nevertheless these buildings are known around the world and their details reflect arts, crafts and materials from many countries. It is well worth looking closer.

Early Theatres in Stratford-upon-Avon

Over the centuries Stratford-upon-Avon has had a variety of public performance spaces and theatres. In the reign of Elizabeth I the Guild Hall, on the ground floor below the King Edward VI schoolroom, saw some of the great London companies of players including those under the patronage of the Queen, the Earl of Leicester and the Earl of Essex.[2] The Market House and the school were also venues for theatrical performances before public entertainments were prohibited during the Civil War.

The first recorded performance of a Shakespeare play in his native town was of *Othello* at the Town Hall in 1746. This was put on in aid of restoration work on the poet's bust in the parish church. There were no plays staged during David Garrick's Jubilee in 1769, but visits by Roger Kemble's company and others from the 1760s to the 1780s included plays in the converted barn at the Unicorn Inn, in Wood Street,[3] and in the Woolsack Inn[4] at 12-14 Bridge Street. Playbills survive from the Theatre, or New Theatre, in a converted timber-framed barn in Chapel Lane, near the site of the Union Club today, and in the early 1820s there was a theatre in the Corporation tithe barn in Windsor Street. This was known as the Henley Street Theatre and stood where the Birthplace coach park is now. In 1821 in Moor Town's End[5] the New Theatre had a classical frontage added to a former barn.[6] Scowton's Theatre, in Rother Market, also hosted occasional entertainments, including circus, in the period 1823-27.

1827 saw the laying of the foundation stone for the Shakespearean Theatre in Chapel Lane. The idea of this theatre had begun with the formation of a Shakespeare Club in 1824. Within three years the club had obtained the patronage of King George IV and a festival was held from 23 to 27 April 1830 in which Charles Kean performed at the renamed Royal Shakespearean Theatre. Other events for this festival were staged in a specially built rotunda in Rother Market. This theatre continued in use until it was purchased in 1872 by James Halliwell-Phillipps who demolished it to develop the Great Garden of New Place.[7]

The Beginnings

Before the Tercentenary of Shakespeare's birth was celebrated in 1864 plans were discussed by committees in Stratford-upon-Avon and in London to decide how a suitable memorial to William Shakespeare should be created. Three ideas were put forward: first for a school of drama to be endowed in London; second for the embellishment of the Shakespeare family properties still existing in Stratford; and third for a statue and monument to be raised either in Stratford or in London.

Edward Flower, founder of Stratford's brewery, was a leader in the plans to celebrate the Tercentenary and the family was a major financial supporter of the events that finally took place in a great timber pavilion put up on part of the land in Southern Lane that Charles Edward, Edward's son, would later purchase when he built his family home, Avonbank. The Tercentenary fortnight, which included a ball, Handel's *Messiah,* banquets and several Shakespeare performances, was a financial disaster[8] and afterwards the pavilion had to be dismantled and sold off. A few years on, to mark the pavilion's memory, Sarah, Mrs. Charles Flower, planted a circle of poplar trees that remained until they became dangerous and were taken down in the 1950s. This site was later used as a tennis court and then as the car park for the first Other Place theatre.[9]

It seemed by 1865 as if no lasting monument to celebrate Shakespeare's three hundred years would survive in his native town. Several locations in Stratford were looked at for a possible shrine and statue of Shakespeare. With the backing of the mayor, James Cox, a design by John Gibbs, an Oxford architect, was selected. His typically Victorian idea of a heavily sculpted vaulted building, in the style but not quite on the scale of London's Albert Memorial, was not generally approved and the suggestion lapsed for lack of funds.[10]

In 1872, following the demolition of the Royal Shakespearean Rooms in Chapel Lane, the vicar, the Reverend J. D. Collis, and a few local gentlemen requested the architect, John Cotton of Birmingham and Bromsgrove, to draw up plans for a permanent theatre for local use to be erected in Chestnut Walk, near where the Broad Street School was later built. The proposals did not please and the plans came to nothing.[11]

The idea of a real memorial, a full scale theatre, took firm hold in the mind of Charles Edward Flower, who joined the staff of Flowers brewery when he was fifteen and eventually succeeded his father, who died in 1883, as head of the firm. It was ten years after the Tercentenary before a scheme for a theatre could be properly considered but in 1874 Charles Edward Flower purchased from Callaway's builder's yard two acres between Waterside and the river edge near the ancient Clopton Bridge. This was very close to the spot where the Rotunda had been erected for the Jubilee in 1769. Now there were canal wharfs and storage sheds alongside, but it was in sight of the church where William Shakespeare was buried. In October of that year Flower proposed to donate this land to the Stratford-upon-Avon Corporation so that a theatre could be built. In February 1875, after discussion with a group of local gentlemen who formed a committee, a letter signed by the Committee's secretary *pro tem*, Charles Edward Flower, stated

> *This is an opportune time for renewing the project which was proposed in 1864 for erecting a suitable Monument to Shakespeare in his native town, and that Monument should take the form of a Memorial Theatre, a building which, inside and out, should be as completely adapted for its object, and as architecturally ornamental as possible.*[12]

On 3 March 1875, Sir Robert North Collie Hamilton, Bart., John James Nason, then Mayor of Stratford, R. M. Bird and R. Gibbs met with Charles Edward Flower and three others at Avonbank. Their first formal minutes as the Council for the Shakespeare Memorial Association recorded their pledge to 'build a small theatre in which to have occasional performances of Shakespeare's plays.' Later, at the Town Hall on 29 March, the Associates decided to be registered under the Companies Act and the Shakespeare Memorial Theatre was born.[13]

R. H. Hobbes, as well as Charles Edward and his brother Edgar, together with James Cox, whose timber yard lay between the Bancroft and the bridge, agreed to issue a call for support and for financial subscriptions. Advance subscriptions, led by an initial £1,000 from Charles Edward himself, soon came to over £2,500.

The First Theatre 1879 - 1926

A competition was launched to attract designs for a theatre with an associated library and picture gallery, to be surrounded by a garden which would be maintained by the Corporation. Details of the competition were sent to thirty-one selected architects as well as to the main architectural journals. They were also sent to theatres in Australia, India and Germany to encourage performances to be given in aid of the project. The first name

1. a) The theatre under construction, March 1879.
(Note the hut retained for scenery storage until 1889.)

b) The completed theatre and picture gallery wing, from the north, 1885.

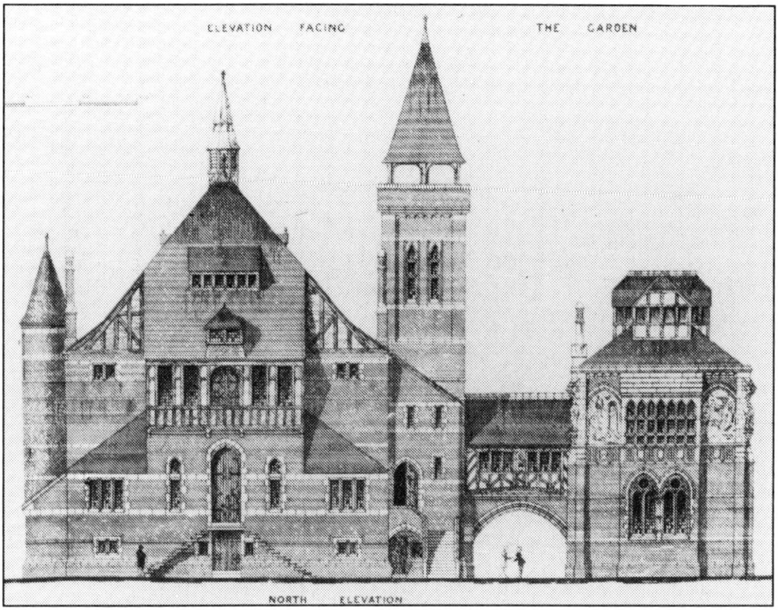

2. a) Unsworth's competition drawing for the proposed theatre and picture gallery. (*Building News* 22 September 1876)

b) Revised architect's drawing of the picture gallery and tower, 1879.

3. The Auditorium

a) 1879

b) from the stage

c) 1920.

4. a) Facade of picture gallery and library wing, 1895.

b) Interior of picture gallery, 1888.

on the list of invitees was Sir George Gilbert Scott but he was not among the 103 people who wrote in seeking application forms.[14]

In February 1876 drawings submitted, anonymously, by twenty-five architects were exhibited for a week in Stratford's Town Hall for public consideration. 'The style and treatment displayed in these designs is as varied as their degrees of excellence', wrote the *Birmingham Daily Post* reporter on 1 March 1876. There were Gothic, Venetian Gothic, Elizabethan, Classical and Palladian examples. Edgar Flower had sent in a drawing of his own, but for many the design labelled 'What here shall miss our toil shall strive to mend' stood out as the 'most original and most quaint'.[15] The local paper found this building 'like a Norman tower with a lamp-shade roof' and preferred the drawings of Messrs. Nightingale and Darbyshire. The efforts of J. and L. Florence were described as 'like a superior Swiss villa' and those of Lee Brothers and Paine had a 'quite inadequate stage'.[16] The *Builder* of 4 March 1878 selected 'What here shall miss' as being 'solid and unpretentious ... ... in spite of some rudeness and roughness of manner ... ... The building is monumental in character'.

The twenty-five designs were also exhibited at the Pump Rooms in nearby Leamington Spa where a public meeting was held, presided over by Lord Leigh and the mayors of both Leamington Spa and Stratford-upon-Avon. Here the drawings were discussed. The *Leamington Spa Courier* [17] picked out 'Our Will' with

> *a simple, inexpensive design which had as its leading feature an open corridor, or gallery looking over the river and which the exhibitor suggested might be utilised by spectators on the occasion of aquatic fetes, fireworks and regattas and form an agreeable lounge for smokers.*

Another of the drawings to cause much comment was that of James, Seward and Thomas, of Cardiff, whose plans showed a large library and reading room at right angles to a theatre of concert hall proportions, to which it was linked by a small arched bridge. The facades of both buildings were elaborately adorned with iconographical sculptures representing Drama, Comedy and Tragedy as well as characters from Shakespeare's plays. These, with a Memorial Tower above an imposing entrance stairway, combined to give the impression of a highly decorated Gothic cathedral. The motto for this design was 'A Deed without a Name'.[18]

The committee, in search of a theatre as a memorial, not a memorial that contained a theatre, selected the five best designs including 'What here shall miss' which had been submitted by William Frederick Unsworth and his twenty-one year old partner, Edward John Dodgshun, whose architectural practice was at 13 Buckingham Street, Strand, in London. At the Leamington meeting their plan was described as

> *a successful attempt at originality of conception in mediaeval design ... ... It had a plain semi-circular auditorium broken on the outside by slight buttresses carrying an overhanging gallery, cresting the walls. Above this a conical roof rises, the whole being somewhat suggestive of Durer's famous round towers at Nuremberg ... ...*[19]

The first drawings of the five finalists were shown again in Stratford Town Hall and the architectural press made its comments. The *Building News'* view of Messrs. Dodgshun and Unsworth's plan was that 'it is certainly not devoid of merit' but felt there was too much straining after the picturesque.[20] The finalists were then asked to submit detailed plans, with new mottos, by 15 May. These would be displayed at Stratford and then at the Royal Dramatic College in London's Regent Street.[21]

The committee of the Shakespeare Association had reserved the right to consult an independent assessor although the *Builder*, on 4 March 1876, had said 'we think the Stratford committee seem to know much better what they are about than competition committees generally do.' The choice was ultimately made with the aid of Edward Middleton Barry, R. A., Professor of Architecture at the Royal Academy who, in 1860, had succeeded his father, Sir Charles Barry, as architect of the Palace of Westminster,[22] and the plan whose motto was now 'But to the purpose and so to the venture' was chosen. This was Dodgshun and Unsworth's plan of which the *Building News* said

> *The revised design retains all the leading points of the first ... ... the only alteration made is that the relative positions of the theatre and the picture gallery are reversed.*[23]

This meant that instead of the gallery being alongside the river as the original drawings showed, the gallery would now be entered directly from the road, opposite the end of Chapel Lane. The winning design, published on 22 September 1876,[24] had a quite different tower from that which was finally to be built, and other exterior decorative details were to change considerably, mainly as a result of expense and fund-raising difficulties in the years to come. *(Pl.2)*

Dodgshun and Unsworth were awarded the 25 guinea prize in July 1876[25] and the firm was contracted to be paid £500 for the theatre plans whether or not the project was completed. The partners moved into larger premises at 2 Great Queen Street, Westminster, and Unsworth, who had a keen interest in the architecture of the past, especially the French Gothic, took over the detail and the supervision of the Shakespeare Memorial Theatre's construction. The partners had worked together for only a short time before entering the theatre plans competition. Edward Dodgshun had trained in his native Leeds and soon after arriving in London had entered into partnership with William Unsworth who was three years his senior. Unsworth, from Bath, where he had been articled to Wilson and Wilcox in 1869, had travelled extensively in France before starting practice in London in 1875.

Once the Memorial Theatre was opened Edward Dodgshun left London to return to Leeds and, in 1898, he became for a short while the partner of Cumberland's county architect, G. Dale Oliver. Dodgshun built Silcoates School at Wakefield and the Crown and Mitre Hotel in Carlisle but most of his later work was domestic. He died in 1927, aged 73.[26] After 1880 William Unsworth's base was to be in Sussex, and later Petersfield, in Hampshire, where he was in partnership with his son and with Harry Inigo Triggs.[27] Among other public buildings Unsworth was to design were the chapel of King's School, Warwick, completed in 1895,[28] and the interior designs for the choir of the chapel of Rossall School in Lancashire. Unsworth died in 1912, aged 61.[29] Both Dodgshun and Unsworth became Fellows of the Royal Institute of British Architects in 1891.

Activity on the Shakespeare Memorial Theatre site began quickly once the architects were selected, and P. Horseman and Company of Wolverhampton set about digging and laying out the foundations under Clerk of Works, J. Mills.[30] It was a difficult, marshy location and the winter weather delayed progress as concrete had to be laid four feet deep instead of the planned three feet. It was not until April 1877 that the main contractor for the building, the firm of W. H. Lascelles of 121 Bunhill Row, London, had its tender accepted. As with Horseman's bid the previous year the committee accepted the lowest estimates submitted to it and Lascelles proposed to complete the main theatre for £9,256, the integral tower for £1,437, and a bridge to connect the building to an art gallery and library wing, which would be built once the theatre was finished, for a further £531.[31]

The foundation stone was laid by Provincial Grand Master Lord Leigh, with full Masonic honours, on 23 April 1877. A dedication speech was made by actor William Creswick with a response by Charles Flower. The ceremony cost £174 0s 7d which was offset by £10 11s 3d collected by 'young ladies' in the watching crowd.[32] Work then pressed ahead under the guidance of Lascelles' Clerk of Works, William R. Smith, and over the next year the building gradually took shape. *(Pl.1a)*

The Association Committee, whose members became the theatre's governors, chose specially made red facing-bricks from Laurence's Works at Bracknell, near Ascot, while the main building material, for economy's sake, was local red brick made at Espley's brickworks in Birmingham Road, Stratford-upon-Avon. The head bricklayer was Henry Narraway, and there was some discussion in the local press that Lascelles was paying its bricklayers London rates of 8d or 8½d an hour which was 2d an hour more than local wages for such work. The brickwork was dressed and ornamented with Bath stone which was at first prepared before being transported to the building site. This delayed progress so stonemasons were taken on to work on the spot. A small spire-like roof-turret was put in place in September 1878 before the roof tiling, in Eureka green slates, was completed. John Nason, Vice-Chairman of the Governors and former Mayor of Stratford-upon-Avon, fixed the final weather-vane on top of the finished theatre in January 1879.[33]

William Unsworth's design was a mixture of Gothic and Tudor detail on a red-brick structure, with Elizabethan style chimneys. On the north side, facing towards Clopton Bridge, half-timbering described by the *Leamington Courier* as 'rustic timbering'[34] was designed to reflect the mixture of timber and brick found in the town.[35] This later created a curious counter effect alongside the red and blue check and striped patterning of the brickwork on the tower, while the pinnacles and turrets of the main building were to earn comparison with a German fairy-tale castle.

There was much controversy in the national press about Stratford's audacity to presume that the classical theatre could sustain an audience outside London, and about the chosen design of the building.

We beg distinctly and indignantly to protest against the whole paltry and impertinent business ... ... They have no mandate to speak in the name of the public or to invest with the attribute of a national undertaking a little mutual admiration club whose object is to endow Stratford-upon-Avon with a spick and span new Elizabethan building to be half theatre and half mechanics institute ... ... The Governors and Council are respectable nobodies ... ... It is an insult to the memory of Shakespeare, ...

wrote the *Daily Telegraph*.[36] Other papers supported the scheme. 'We see no reason why Stratford, especially with its summer assemblage of Shakespearian pilgrims, should not support a theatre', said the *Birmingham Daily Gazette*.[37] In October 1877 a public meeting was held to refute the opposition and to encourage subscriptions to the project. Charles Flower was described soon after this in *Funny Folks* satirical paper as 'Self-Raising Flower' as he had by now given more than £4,000 to the scheme.[38]

There was prominent backing for the project, nevertheless, from actors such as Samuel Phelps, William Creswick and Barry Sullivan, who was to be the first Festival Director. The *Daily Telegraph* remained an opponent and even as the theatre neared completion in March 1879 it was critical of the 'high sounding scheme', to which the *Stratford-upon-Avon Herald* replied that this was 'unjust and ungentlemanly'.[39]

Stratford's new theatre would be seen from all sides as it stood on the bank of the River Avon and would be fronted by an ornamental pool converted from one of the old canal basins of the Bancroft meadow. The critics who spoke against the design were familiar only with theatres on small city or town sites, hemmed in by other buildings. Few people had the vision of Charles Edward Flower who saw what could be done to create a picturesque as well as a practical home for the performance of Shakespeare's plays. There was no intention of having plays performed for more than a few weeks in a spring festival each year. At other times the building would provide a venue for local events as well as a museum and library for the study of Shakespeare.

The Shakespeare Memorial Theatre was conceived in two parts, the first of which comprised the auditorium, stage and dressing rooms, with a tower

113 feet high that contained offices below a water tank for emergency use in the event of fire.[40] Later would come a library and art gallery wing. In the end the theatre was built first and the second building was completed in 1881. It was connected to the theatre by a half-timbered and roofed arch-bridge of brick which reached over a carriage-way, while the tower was delayed for two more years.

A Shakespeare Memorial Library was to be housed in two rooms on the wing's ground floor from which a York stone stairway led up to a saloon. The stairs were flanked by stained glass lancet windows showing the 'Seven Ages of Man'. These windows can still be seen and admired, especially since a redecoration scheme was completed in the winter of 1991-92. Local glass and stone-carving craftmen's skills were also employed elsewhere in the building.

There was access across the bridge at first floor level to the theatre's dress circle. Once the wing was completed the staircase would provide the principal entrance through the saloon to the best seats in the auditorium. From the saloon, a stone and wrought-iron balustraded landing opened into a 25-foot-high, glass-roofed hall to house a picture gallery. Edgar Flower supervised the hanging of the first loan exhibition of paintings which opened in April 1881.[41] There was space for a museum of Shakespeariana in a further room at the far end. This was later to be named the Benson Room in honour of Sir Frank Benson whose acting company staged the annual Shakespeare Festivals from 1886 to 1918. *(Pl.4b)*

Ornamental brickwork and timbering provided the decorative features on the exterior of the theatre, while the library and picture gallery eventually displayed the art of the sculptor and artist in the gargoyles and other Gothic detail of the corners and window frames inspired by the fairies in *A Midsummer Night's Dream*. The main entrance had a Juliet balcony over steep York stone steps leading to carved oak doors. Above the library's oriel windows were three panels prepared to receive further decoration. The terracotta panels that were placed here in 1885 were modelled by German sculptor Paul Kummer.[42] One panel representing history, which showed the Hubert and Prince Arthur scene from *King John*, was presented by the theatre's architect W. F. Unsworth. The actress Mary Anderson gave the £100 proceeds of a benefit performance of *As You Like It* in August 1885 to pay for both the tragedy panel of Hamlet beside Yorick's grave and the comedy panel with Rosalind, disguised as Ganymede, persuading Orlando to woo her in the Forest of Arden, from *As You Like It. (Pl.4a)*

Many of the exterior ornament details of the library and picture gallery wing can still be seen today. Above the terracotta panels there are four tall niches of stone which, it was suggested in 1882, 'might have sculptures as gifts from those desirous of connecting their names with some special portion of the Memorial'. The niches have remained empty ever since.[43]

Inside the Shakespeare Memorial Library the first room of bookstacks had a fireplace of highly decorated Caen stone with Purbeck marble columns. A room at the far end with oak panelling had a carved oak overmantle with a Shakespeare portrait decoration. This room served as a reading room and librarian's office, from which a separate small side door led to the street. The chief carpenter for the building was W. Cooper but the names of the sculptor for the library stone fireplace and a second one in the gallery above were not recorded.[44]

In 1881 there were discussions among the Governors as to whether decoration and interior painting of the theatre should be carried out before the tower was built. They decided 'it is most desirous that no time should be lost in the completion of the tower and watertank.'[45] The tower was eventually approved in 1882 and was described as the 'crowning feature to the work and will give a proper effect to the whole building.'[46] The architect had modified his original ideas for the tower. Its brick and stonework now had decorative stripes below a bold check pattern, and, instead of the competition-winning 'lamp-shade' design, there were four small turrets around a central roof. Near the top there was a deeply recessed gallery which gave fine views across the town and the surrounding countryside.

The tower was built in 1883 under Superintendent of Works, Mr. Braid, and was completed when Edgar Flower braved a high wind to put an elegant weathervane in place on 19 October 1883.[47] The local paper admired the workmanship: 'there being a stability about everything which means an existence of some hundreds of years.'[48] The tower was the last part of the main building to be completed and gave 'the whole the character of a monument'.[49] *(Pl.1b)*

To complete the group of buildings associated with the new theatre there was a porter's lodge, to the south of the steps up to the picture gallery. This was constructed by Smallwood and Company in 1885. According to the *Stratford-upon-Avon Chronicle*:[50] 'When completed [the porter's lodge] will form a very handsome addition to the main buildings, and will greatly add to the picturesque appearance of the noble pile.' The end of work on the lodge gateway and the fencing around the south gardens was reported to the Governors at their meeting on 28 April 1886, by which time the south gardens had also been cleared and levelled.[51] The gateway was severely damaged in 1973 when a French tourist coach collided with it, but it was restored and today is a fitting feature alongside the stone path up to the Swan Theatre's main doors.

An attractive garden was gradually laid out in the 1880s as finances allowed. The Corporation's purchase from the Great Western Railway of three acres of land, alongside the old canal wharves, was delayed until July 1883 but when this was done the local paper had exhorted the town to make a worthy surrounding to the theatre.[52] Slowly, to the north of the theatre, a water garden reminiscent of manor house gardens in other parts of Warwickshire was completed. It remained until the Bancroft ornamental lake was finally drained in 1901.[53] In October 1886 a special meeting of the Borough Council recorded its thanks to Charles Flower for paying the whole of the remaining cost of laying out the Bancroft property. This relieved the rate payers of further expense in the creation of the riverside gardens.[54] The gardens were completed by the following May 'to form as a whole an agreeable surrounding to the Memorial Building'[55] and the town held a formal opening of the Bancroft gardens on Queen Victoria's Jubilee day, 21 June 1887.

The final addition to the landscaping of the theatre was the setting up of Lord Ronald Sutherland Gower's Shakespeare Monument in the garden to the south of the theatre. Letters of advice on the positioning of the Gower Monument were received from Charles Flower's nephew, the architect Arthur Smyth Flower.[56] It was eventually unveiled by Lady Hodgson, wife of the Mayor, Sir Arthur Hodgson, in October 1888,[57] and was the focal point of a lawned garden with open views of the river and the parish church beyond. Later that month 'vandalism by children and mischievous persons' necessitated the closure of the theatre gardens to all except those who held tickets to view the theatre and picture gallery. The public was to be admitted only on Sundays in future, when a park superintendent would be on duty.[58]

The theatre buildings inspired such comments as: 'the treatment is solid and the effect picturesque; and the building is monumental in character without that feature being allowed to interfere with convenience and suitability in arrangement';[60] 'When the gardens have been developed the memorial will no doubt have one of the most attractive positions ever accorded to a playhouse'.[61] At the unveiling of the Gower Monument Oscar Wilde called the theatre 'a beautiful building, one of the loveliest erected in England in many years'.[62] Fifty years later tastes in architecture had changed and the theatre historians M. Day and J. C. Trewin wrote in 1932: 'Certainly the theatre was not beautiful. Its gables and pinnacles worried the eye. It lacked simplicity of line. It had none of Stratford's essential dignity.'[63]

The theatre's construction finally cost about £11,000. The library and picture gallery with the tower cost a further £9,000 and the gardens were additional later expenses. Charles Flower chose not to reveal the full extent of his personal contributions but in April 1886 the Governors recorded a vote of thanks in their annual meeting minutes

> *to Mr. Charles Edward Flower for his munificent gift of £22,700 together with the free grant of the land on which the building and gardens are situated and to express a hearty feeling of congratulation that, thanks to Mr. Flower's liberality, the Memorial buildings and gardens are finished and out of debt.*

Charles Flower responded to this vote of thanks by donating 'all those buildings and cottages on the opposite side of the street to the theatre, the rents to be devoted to the maintenance of the [theatre] building.'[64]

The theatre had virtually been paid for by Charles Edward Flower. Subscriptions had come in from many supporters and those who gave over £100 were created Governors of the Memorial Association; but compared with Flower's money the gifts were small. The largest donations from individuals came from leading actors such as Henry Irving who gave £120 and Barry Sullivan who gave 100 guineas. The American actor, Edwin Booth, and Heinrich Schliemann, the archaeologist, were among those whose names appeared on the final subscription list.[65]

'The Play's the Thing'

The interior of the theatre was of a more conventional nature than its controversial outward appearance. Economy would not allow ornate gold and plush decoration but the auditorium was compact and comfortable.

The Times reported on 25 April 1879 'in decoration and appointment it is quite up to the standard of the metropolis'. The walls of the theatre were on average 3 feet thick and the roof was supported on massive wrought-iron principal beams. All public stairways were of York stone, with ornamental iron balustrades. The woodwork throughout the interior was of Christiana yellow pine with dado framing for the orchestra pit, stalls and gallery of the auditorium. Above the audience hung a great 'sunburner' of 250 gas lights. This was supplied by Messrs. Strode and Company, art metal workers, of Osnaburgh Street, near Regent's Park in London.

The auditorium looked not unlike a non-conformist chapel with its horse-shoe shaped dress circle enfolding the proscenium arch which was 26 feet wide by 27 feet 6 inches high.[66] On the ground floor there were fifty-three orchestra stalls from amongst which rose wrought iron girders and brick piers to support a dress circle of 158 seats. Above this was a gallery, reached by a separate outside staircase from the street alongside the carriage way. The gallery and pit benches together could accommodate 500 unreserved seats. The upper walls of the auditorium had clerestory windows with window seats in front of them. When painting and decoration was completed in 1885 a quotation was added, encircling the horseshoe at ceiling level with the words: 'The poet's pen turns them to shapes and gives to airy nothing a local habitation and a name', from *A Midsummer Night's Dream. (Pl.3a,b)*

The audience's view of the stage was altered in 1913 when the original blue Hornton stone pillars either side of the proscenium were removed and the ornamental carved arch was lowered to create a rectangular frame 19 feet high. At the same time the orchestra pit was lowered to put an end to unnecessary blocking of sight-lines from the pit benches which had been a problem from the beginning. *(Pl.3c)*

The stage lay behind an ornate drop-cloth depicting Queen Elizabeth I arriving in state at the Globe Theatre in Shakespeare's London. This cloth was painted by W. R. Beverley, and was repaired in 1895. It had to be restored with partial repainting in 1903 by S. Lawson Booth. The stage, behind the curtain, was 53 feet 2 inches wide and 48 feet 8 inches deep. It was laid and fitted by Mr. Owen of London.[67] The grid for flying scenery was 46 feet above the stage floor, while the basement floor level was 18 feet below the stage. There were seven dressing rooms, with the ladies on the west and the gentlemen on the east, or riverbank side. These rooms were reached by perilous spiral metal staircases up to their mezzanine floor. Only dressing-room one was at stage level, for the star performer, on stage left. At the back of the stage was a small property store, and an equally small green room, which, nevertheless, was a space for actors to relax between calls or to meet informally at other times.

After a ballot[68] had been held for first-night seats, the theatre was opened as the focal point of the town's traditional celebrations of Shakespeare's birthday, on a pouring wet 23 April 1879, with a performance of *Much Ado About Nothing* in which Barry Sullivan and Helen Faucit played the leading roles. The invalid Sarah Flower attended the performance in her bath chair and was carried to her seat beside her husband in the dress circle for this long awaited occasion.[69] *The Times* gave a column to describing the Birthday celebrations and the new theatre building which was described as 'small but compact, handsome, almost perfect', but of the performance the paper said only that it was 'conscientiously performed to the manifest pleasure of the audience'. The *Daily Telegraph* saw the building had 'elegant proportions and striking features'. This critic disliked the brickwork contrast of the 'scarlet and white and parallel bands of striking black and white' but felt 'time will tone down the glare'. Otherwise the national press paid little attention but the *Daily Telegraph* sounded a prophetic note when its reporter wrote:

> *doubtless in time other artists will follow Miss Helen Faucit upon these boards and within Shakespeare's town [they will] produce his plays in an admirable style year by year.*[70]

It was the beginning of an annual homage to William Shakespeare that has grown to the ten-month celebration that is upheld by the Royal Shakespeare Company today.

From the first festival of 1879 alterations were made to the theatre as practicalities required. Three rows of seats were added in front of the pit in October 1880 to create orchestra stalls.[71] More pit seating was added in 1899. The dress circle was modified in 1903-4 with wider gangways when attention was being paid to fire safety measures. At the same time the dress circle upholstery was changed from leather to velvet plush.[72] In 1886, after the gardens had been completed and Charles Flower had made arrangements for the future maintenance of the theatre, he also proposed that two cottages on Waterside should be demolished at his expense and a scene dock built to allow the removal of 'the ugly building standing by the theatre', - by which he meant a wooden shed that remained on the river bank.[73]

Arthur Smyth Flower, who practised as an architect in Aldeburgh, Suffolk,[74] was asked by his uncle to design the scenery dock together with a lecture room. This simple building of local brick with blue lias stone had Campden stone facings to the windows and doors that fronted Waterside, opposite the stage end of the theatre. Above a tall entrance that would allow the trucks of scenery to be wheeled straight in, the gable was of tarred fir and rough cast. Behind lay a lecture room 53 feet by 27 feet, with a moveable stage and two small dressing rooms at one end, and a gallery at the other. The building was constructed by a local builder, G. Whateley of 27 Rother Street, and cost £757. It was a gift to the theatre from Charles Flower and, after completion in 1889, was soon in use, providing much needed storage space, and a club for theatre visitors in the season. The hall was also available for hire for local events.[75]

Arthur S. Flower later worked on other buildings in Stratford-upon-Avon. In 1892 he supervised restoration work at King Edward VI Grammar School,[76] and he worked on restoration at the Church Street almshouses between 1897 and 1902. He was also responsible for the plans for the Technical College built in Henley Street in 1899-1900, which is now part of the public library.

Drainage was improved in the theatre's basement in 1898, after which costume preparation-space and wardrobe storage were placed there. In this same year the scenery grooves, now very old-fashioned, were removed from the stage and electric light was installed in the dress circle. Gas lighting remained for the stage and orchestra pit until 1907 as this was considered to be more flexible for performance use. 'New fittings for the working of the scenery on stage and other modern improvements' were also made in 1907.[77] Nothing could be done, however, to alleviate the difficulties of setting from the flies which were surrounded by the peaks and gables of the roof.

Once the festival became established the theatre was the annual home of the Benson Company for many years, and when William Bridges-Adams took over the running of the festivals in 1919 he found a warm and friendly atmosphere where 'the horse-shoe tiers take the stage, as it were, in their embrace, the play's magnetism runs round the house in an unbroken circuit.'[78]

The theatre Governors were always aware of the potential problem of fire. As early as 1882 there were trials with asbestos paint, as the *Stratford-upon-Avon Herald* reported, 'so that the Memorial Theatre can be made almost perfectly secure against fire.'[79] For safety's sake all doors in the building had been made to open outwards, except the main doors which had Smith's patent hinges to allow them to swing either way.[80] Then, in 1880, a self-acting pump was installed by Ball and Horton, engineers of Stratford-upon-Avon, for a continuous supply of water from the river to the tank above which the tower was built three years later.[81]

In 1898-99 an outside iron escape staircase was built by the St. Pancras Iron Company. It led from the dress circle and was described in the 1899 annual report as 'of the plainest description in order to be as inconspicuous as possible', while an inside staircase was added for the gallery patrons on the east side of the building. Further precautions were taken in 1903 when a fireproof curtain was installed on the stage behind the Beverley drop-curtain. An outside staircase from the gallery was constructed by Ball and Horton in 1904-5, with a wrought iron balustrade crafted by septuagenarian John Cranmer, to a design by architect W. F. Unsworth. On 28 April 1905 the *Stratford-upon-Avon Herald* reported 'the Memorial Theatre is now the safest building of its kind in the kingdom', and for twenty years this seemed to be the case.

At 2.45 in the afternoon of 6 March 1926 smoke was seen coming from the theatre. It was a few weeks before the new season was due to begin and no-one was in the building at the time. Fire engines from as far away as Warwick came to assist in fighting the blaze, but all was in vain. The flames were fed by the costumes and scenery stored below the stage and the tower became a tall chimney. In the early evening the auditorium roof fell in and by next morning only a blackened shell remained around twisted girders; through the ruined doorway was seen the outline of Gower's Lady Macbeth wringing her hands in sorrow.

The library and art gallery had been saved from the fire as a human chain had passed the books and paintings across Waterside to the lecture room and the fire fighters had prevented the flames leaping the bridge to the adjacent gallery. This building was to be carefully preserved despite controversy in the 1930s about its retention, and fifty years later it came into its own once more when the RSC Collection became the main approach to the Swan Theatre.

The New Theatre 1932

At the Shakespeare Birthday luncheon in 1925 one of the theatre's Governors, playwright George Bernard Shaw, criticised Stratford's Victorian theatre building which was nearing its fiftieth anniversary. 'The Memorial is an admirable building, adapted for every conceivable purpose except that of a theatre ... ... Stratford wants a new theatre.' Within a year this wish had unexpectedly become practicable.

Despite all the efforts to make it fireproof the theatre had been destroyed and the cause of the fire was never discovered although speculation blamed an electrical fault, or a careless cigarette end left when the building had been in use that morning. There was no question in the minds of the people involved, however, but that the Shakespeare festival must continue. Two days later Archibald Flower, nephew of the founder and now Chairman of the Governors made it clear that there had already been discussion following recent criticism of Unsworth's building.

> *We had gone so far as to get plans out for a new theatre on another site, intending to use the old one for concerts, etc. We could not very well pull the old one down, but now that road has been cleared for us the old one provides an ideal site for such a modern theatre as we want.*[82]

The morning after the disaster Archibald Flower began to organise a temporary theatre. The Stratford Picture House, built in 1912 in Greenhill Street, had remained in the theatre's control since its purchase by the Flower family in 1923 to accommodate equipment that was no longer required to show films at the theatre in the winter months.[83] The Picture House had a small stage which William Bridges-Adams, who had directed the festivals since 1919, realised had possibilities, and plans were swiftly drawn up. Within six weeks dressing rooms were built behind and alongside the Picture House, and an extension was added to the rear of the stage. The 1926 season opened on time in April and the festivals were held at the cinema building for the next few years.

Meanwhile a fund was set up to raise money for a new Memorial Theatre. The appeal was launched on 26 March 1926 by the *Daily Telegraph*, the same paper that had been so scathing in 1879 about the probability of success for so provincial an enterprise.[84] Signatories to the appeal included Stanley Baldwin, Ramsey Macdonald and Thomas Hardy. George Bernard

Shaw was one of the first to contribute 100 guineas and other Governors soon followed suit. Before building plans could begin Archibald Flower decided that as much expert advice as possible should be sought and in April 1926 he invited representatives of the worlds of finance, art, literature, architecture and drama to form an advisory panel.[85] Those asked were Reginald McKenna, Chairman of the Midland Bank, Sir Charles Holmes, Director of the National Gallery, James Barrie, the dramatist, E. Guy Dawber, President of the Royal Institute of British Architects, and Harley Granville-Barker.

Granville-Barker, the distinguished Shakespeare director and literary critic, was adamant that if he gave his time to the advisory committee it should serve a useful purpose and his word would be heeded. (He may perhaps have been aware of Archie Flower's reputation for preferring committees of two, of which one member was usually unavailable for meetings.)[86] In an occasionally acerbic correspondence with Archie Flower over the next few months Granville-Barker attempted to curb the enthusiastic aims of the Chairman to achieve a large and decorative building for the new theatre.

The first point to be decided in the spring of 1926 was the site for the new Shakespeare Memorial Theatre. The two alternatives were adjacent to the ruins of the burnt-out building by the river, or on part of the garden area of the theatre founder's house, Avonbank, which was now used as the parish vicarage. Writing to Granville-Barker on 20 April, Archie Flower described the choice of site as 'a difficult National question.'[87]

Avonbank's kitchen garden on Southern Lane was the site of the Tercentenary pavilion of 1864 and this location had the advantage that a theatre there would be viewed only from the front or road direction. Such a building would be much cheaper as it would not need to be designed for viewing from all sides in the way the riverside site required. Also 'a beautiful clear approach could be made' through the vicarage gardens with a river frontage, to provide an adequate decorative surrounding. 'The orangery', thought Granville-Barker, could be 'a perfectly appropriate gallery of Shakespearean performers in the eighteenth century.'[88] (The orangery remains in the theatre's gardens today, where it has been used for a number of years as a brass-rubbing centre.)

By June the advisory committee had decided the Tercentenary site was the preferred position for a new theatre to seat between 800 and 1,000 people, and the ruins of the old Shakespeare Memorial should be converted, it suggested, into a conference hall for the town's use. The committee agreed[89] that a competition should be held to select an architect, from among British and American entrants. The prize would be £1,000, and a panel of assessors to make the final choice would be led by E. Guy Dawber.[90] Taking advice from W. Bridges-Adams about the stage requirements, Dawber began to draw up preliminary plans and a guide for the competition. The heavy loss incurred by the first season in the temporary festival theatre at the cinema did not daunt the Governors' plans. In 1926 visitors to the Shakespeare Birthplace Trust properties were 66% down compared with 1925, for this was the year of the General Strike. It was firmly expected that future festivals would achieve improved audience figures.

The Stratford-upon-Avon Corporation did not like the suggestion of the Tercentenary site for the new theatre. It strongly preferred the riverside position despite the comments of Harley Granville-Barker and others that there would be much extra expense in an 'all-round building' and severe problems with foundations so close to the Avon. 'All question of cost apart, the river site ... ... is the finest one', conceded Granville-Barker in October. The recommendations of the advisory committee were published in a memorandum to the theatre Governors clearly stating that the Tercentenary site was preferred 'together with the garden frontage on the river.'[91] Despite the committee's opposition Archie Flower sided with the town councillors and decided the Governors could accept the responsibility for the extra costs and the riverside site was chosen before revised drafts for the competition to find an architect went ahead.

The instructions to architects, issued with the competition advertisement, stated that 'the promoters desire a building simple, beautiful, convenient - a monument worthy of its purpose.' It was suggested that the stage should back onto the former theatre's stage and the Gower Monument might be moved to a new position once the surrounding gardens were laid out to new plans, for which suggestions were also invited. In recognition of the new age of transportation, provision for a theatre car park was described as 'desirable'.

William Bridges-Adams, as director of the festival's theatre company, was consulted about the interior design for the auditorium and the backstage areas. In the event, however, his suggestions for all but the stage were largely discounted when the competition outline was published, as the Governors did not wish to be too precise and so restrict the hand of potential applicants. It was proposed that the theatre seating capacity should be about a thousand, probably in two tiers with a few boxes, including a royal box with its adjacent anteroom.[92] It was later made clear that 'two-tier' meant a ground floor, with a dress circle and a gallery (or balcony) above.

The auditorium should provide for the occasional use of an apron stage in front of the proscenium and there should be an orchestra pit. Sight lines should allow for all seats to be able to see at least 12 feet of stage floor in front of the proscenium arch, and no seat should be closer to the arch than 15 feet nor further than 75 feet from it. The stage should be wide enough to accommodate spacious wings either side 'but a wide proscenium is not desirable'. There must be at least a 50 foot depth of stage and the floor of the acting area should be flat, not raked. The flies should be about 22 feet from the stage floor, which should be completely removable in block units. Further notes of requirements listed dressing rooms, a green room for actors' refreshment, a wardrobe area and workrooms. It seemed to many a great deal to ask of a very compact and rather narrow site. George Bernard Shaw's comment was: 'I do not expect an ideal theatre to be built; I merely want to see a good, working theatre.'[93]

The competition was launched in January 1927 and by November designs from three American and three British architects had been selected from among over seventy detailed submissions. As the Royal Institute was to oversee the competition the final choice lay with assessors E. Guy Dawber and Robert Atkinson. They were to have been joined by the President of the American Academy of Design, Cass Gilbert, but in the end the distinguished American architect Raymond Hood stood in for him.[94] The finalists from America were Robert O. Derrick, of Detroit; Albert J. Rousseau of Ann Arbor, Michigan; and the partners, Albert R. Mohr and Benjamin Moscowitz of New York City. Their designs stood beside those of the London-based architects: D. F. Martin-Smith; the firm of Percy Tubbs Son and Duncan with Rowland Pierce; and Elisabeth Scott.

The three American finalist designs comprised a stone mausoleum from Rousseau, a romantic castellated monastery from Derrick, and a brick and stone cathedral, with two domed towers reminiscent of Charlecote gatehouse, from Mohr and Moscowitz. The Rousseau building had an art-deco cinema-style auditorium, Derrick had a Tudor stage, while Mohr and Moscowitz had an open-air conference hall and a small second auditorium in the attic. Of the British selection Tubbs, Duncan and Pierce had an almost circular auditorium in a massive brick building above a stone cliff rising from the river. Martin-Smith's design had tall oriel windows in a bare otherwise undetailed factory-like brick structure with a huge fly tower dwarfing an incongruously roofed north elevation. A wide avenue approached this across the Bancroft to end at a statue in the midst of a traffic circle like that at London's Victoria monument in the Mall. None of these plans gave much thought to public refreshment areas, or to the practical needs of a working theatre such as back-stage wings and scene dock space. All placed some emphasis on the conference hall conversion as an integral part of their plans.[95]

After deliberation the assessors chose the entry submitted by twenty-nine year-old Elisabeth Scott, the daughter of a Bournemouth doctor.[96] Miss Scott's second cousin was Sir Giles Gilbert Scott, architect of Liverpool Anglican Cathedral and a wide range of other public buildings.[97] She was also great niece of Sir George Gilbert Scott, who had designed London's St. Pancras Station and the Albert Memorial among other prominent Victorian buildings. Elisabeth Scott had gained her diploma from the Architectural Association after five years of study and had worked in Welwyn Garden City before joining Maurice Chesterton's firm in Hampstead. *(Pl.5)*

On receipt of the award Elisabeth Scott went into partnership with her employer, Maurice Chesterton, and to complete the theatre contract, they were joined by John C. Shepherd, the architect fiancé of Alison Sleigh, friend and former fellow student of Elisabeth Scott. Miss Scott had drawn up her ideas for the Shakespeare Memorial Theatre in consultation with Alison Sleigh, with some help and advice from John C. Shepherd. An obituary was to state in 1972: 'In the partnership Scott provided the initiative, Chesterton the administration and Shepherd the flair.'[98]

In her acceptance of the award the architect stated:

> *I belong to the modernist school of architects. By that I mean I believe the function of the building to be the most important thing to be considered. In terms of theatre ... ... this means ... ... that acoustics and sight lines must come first ... ... At the same time I have taken full advantage of the exceptionally beautiful site on the banks of the Avon ... ...*[99]

I have aimed at creating an atmosphere of space and ease. In addition to the ordinary structural necessities there will be ample foyers which will help in impressing the public that they have come to a place where they can for a time forget the outside world.[100]

Once more George Bernard Shaw had a comment: 'although the architect is a woman, hers was the only plan which showed any theatre sense.'[101] In fact, as Professor A. E. Richardson was to point out in the *Builder*: 'This was the first important work erected in this country from the designs of a woman architect.' Later the *Lady* was to record that 'Miss Scott's theatre will stand as a landmark in the professional and artistic achievements of women.'[102] It is worth remembering that the competition year was significant for British women in another way as it was in 1928 that the female voting age was first lowered from thirty to be equal with men at twenty-one.[103]

The assessors issued a report on the competition in November 1927 and stated that the chosen design had

a largeness and simplicity of handling which no other design possesses. The general silhouette and modelling to fit the lines of the river are picturesque and the character of the design shows consideration for the locality.[104]

The only major alteration the assessors recommended, which the Governors immediately approved, was that, instead of white concrete for the exterior, which Elisabeth Scott had thought would echo the Cotswold stone of the Town Hall in nearby Sheep Street, the main building material should be brick which would 'be warmer and more in harmony with the general aspect of the town.'[105] Below the brick, Hornton stone, from the Edgehill quarries a few miles from Stratford, was to be used for the base and plinths, while surrounding terraces were to be York stone with Hornton facings.

Elisabeth Scott had ignored the Gothic and Tudor influences of the first theatre. Nor had she been tempted by the idea of a marble palace of art and culture which other architect competitors had tried to realise. She chose clear, precise, modern lines with curves and strong flowing movement in metal and brickwork. In her work the architect had considered theatres designed by A. and G. Perret in France and by Max

Lettman and Oskar Kauffman in Germany, as well as the Pasadena Theatre in the United States. There were few contemporary British examples, apart from cinemas, which could be useful to her. 'The Stratford site offers difficulties and opportunities', she said as she undertook the task of completing the project.[106]

The architect was allowed twelve months from the award date to prepare her detailed plans. During this time she toured in France and Germany in the company of William Bridges-Adams, and with Archibald Flower and his wife. They looked at specialist features and the latest equipment in theatres wherever they went, especially as Bridges-Adams wanted Elisabeth Scott to allow for as much potential variation as possible behind the scenes for a wide range of presentation methods in the new theatre. 'The need is for absolute flexibility, it should be, so to speak, a box of tricks out of which the childlike mind of the producer may create what shape it pleases', said Bridges-Adams, whose own interests in modern lighting techniques had characterised much of his work in the old theatre.[107]

The choice of Elisabeth Scott's designs and their subsequent development did not go unchallenged by theatre professionals. Terence Gray, who ran the Cambridge Festival Theatre from 1926 to 1933, was outspoken against the choice of a proscenium arch stage:

> *Shakespeare's plays were essentially three dimensional and were intended to be performed in immediate contact with the audience. Not less than one quarter of the acting area [should] be in the auditorium and surrounded by spectators.*

Gray's advice was presented in the *Bookman's Journal* in 1928, when he warned of the dangers of adopting too many mechanical innovations from Germany which were, in any case, already becoming out-dated, and traditionalist producers in England would ignore them.[108] Gray also advocated a single-tier, semi-circular stepped auditorium rather than the fan-shaped three levels of Scott's designs. It was to be another forty years before the Olivier Theatre at the National Theatre would be designed on the lines of Terence Gray's ideas.

Following the suggestion of the competition assessors that 'the Governors should employ an independent expert in theatrical equipment,' further advice on stage facilities, and on sound and light equipment was received

5. a) Elisabeth Scott's winning design 1927.

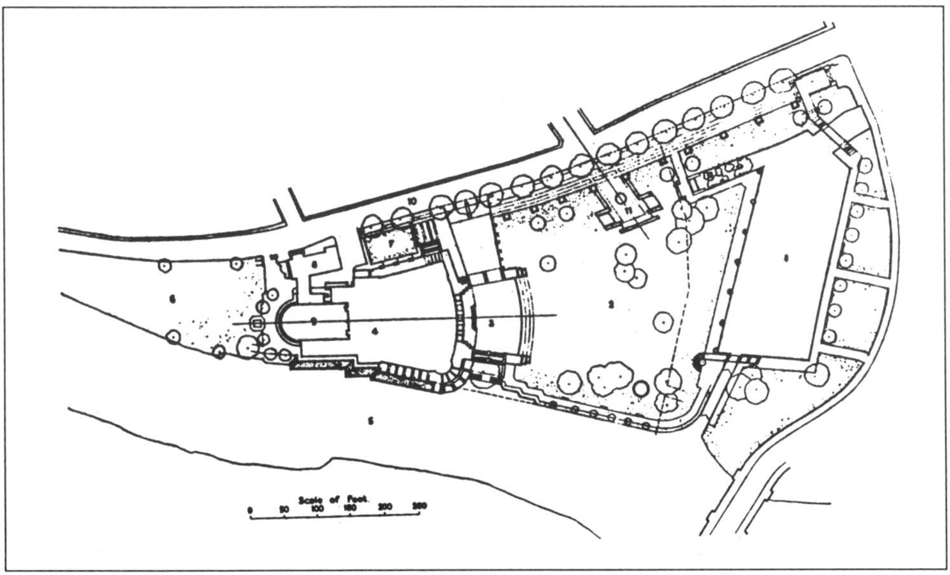

b) Elisabeth Scott's drawing of the site, 1932.

6. River view: *a)* looking south 1932.

b) In 1954 after completion of Balcony refreshment room (1936), Restaurant and River Room (1938) and Dressing Rooms and Green Room (1950-51).

7. Foyer: *a)* 1932.

b) 1972 (Note extended Box Office and small bookstall.)

8. a) Stalls bar and refreshment room, 1932 (Note: ceiling clouds remain in 1993)

b) Dress circle foyer 1954 (Note: light fittings survive in 1993)

from Sir Barry Jackson, with his Birmingham Repertory Theatre and Malvern Festival experience, from stage designer, Norman Wilkinson, and from Russian stage director and designer, Theodore Komisarjevsky. Hope Bagenal gave advice on acoustics and Harold Ridge was brought in as consulting electrical engineer.[109]

It was not for lack of consideration that much professional theatre advice was forgotten or ignored in the final building. Once construction began, the work had to continue through the winter months when the professional theatre practitioners were not on hand in Stratford. The Shakespeare festivals ran from March to September each season in the temporary theatre at the Picture House, but Bridges-Adams was often away in the winter with plays touring in America to raise money for the new theatre. Archie Flower, or in his absence his brother Spenser, and Elisabeth Scott frequently had to make decisions in a hurry, and expense was always at the back of the Chairman's mind. The detailed plan for the exterior views and the public 'front-of-house' areas of the building was much as the architect had submitted to the competition with slight revisions to the access stairs for the balcony and the elimination of boxes from the back of the stalls; but back-stage many amendments were to lead to future problems.

THE BUILDING

The material finally selected for the Shakespeare Memorial Theatre's exterior walls was red-sand bricks made by the Sussex Brick Company. The impact of this was softened by interspersed patterns of silver-grey bricks, hand-made by S. and E. Collier's Company. Hydro-lime was used instead of cement for the brickwork to eliminate the danger of efflorescence on the outer walls later.[110] The main feature of the theatre building, around which it was constructed, was a bold tower above the stage to fit in with Bridges-Adams' request in 1926 for 'great height for flying cloths out of sight, and depth for bridges.'[111] In writing to Granville-Barker of this request in 1928 Archie Flower stated his firm belief: 'The executive and subscribers agree that we should aim at the most complete theatre possible - that nothing but the best is good enough for Shakespeare.' *(Pl.6a)*

The face of the fly tower was not disguised but was made a feature. Patterned with paler bricks, it rose like the funnel of a great ocean liner moored alongside the river. The wall was much admired by J. C. Squire, who wrote: 'At the back, outside, there is one of the finest brick walls ever built. At the top of it there is a little play with vertical mouldings ... ... It is a noble thing.' [112]

Apart from the varied use of brickwork there was little external decoration except for five sculpture panels carved *in situ* out of the bricks at the top of the main north wall above the entrance to the foyer. The sculptor for this was forty-two year-old Eric Kennington who had studied art at Lambeth and Kennington. His first sculpture had been a war memorial in Battersea Park, London, to the 24th Division of Kennington, with whom he had served in 1914. His huge memorial to 'The Missing' was completed at Soissons in France in 1928, before he was asked to work on Elisabeth Scott's building. For the Shakespeare Memorial Theatre Kennington created carvings to depict some of the emotions in Shakespeare's plays: 'Treachery', 'Jollity', 'Martial Ardour', 'Love' and 'Life triumphing over Death'. He said that his work was inspired by the calendar carvings on Chartres cathedral. J. C. Squire wrote of the finished carvings for the theatre that he found them 'inconspicuous and mysterious'.[113] Today they remain clear and are little weathered by time, but they are difficult to see from below as modern flag poles obscure the view. *(Pl.12)*

The illusion of streamlined height for the theatre was carried through around the windows to the north and west with dark Hornton stone linings held in place by bronze studs. Richard Crittall and Company, the London firm of metal window designers, were subcontracted to the architects for all the window frames. Their draughtsman was Roy da Cunha[114] and his designs were executed by Henry Hope and Sons who also created the exterior handrails on terraces and alongside steps leading up from the road. These details were carefully integrated into the overall exterior view of the building, and most remain today.

To the south of the theatre, on the river side, was a pillared loggia accessible only from the terrace. This was intended to hide the burnt-out ruins of the old theatre from the river view. Built into the loggia wall was the foundation stone of the first Memorial Theatre and the loggia ceiling was 'daringly and beautifully' painted by Eric Kennington.[115] For the loggia Gordon Russell designed metal-slatted armchairs for the use of passers-by on a summer's day. In front of the foyer doors was a small area for cars to approach and park and Miss Scott had plans for wide walkways beside the Bancroft gardens leading towards the bridge and the town, as well as a river terrace with a landing stage of steps leading up to the theatre's forecourt.

Sketches for the layout of the Bancroft provided by the architects in March 1931, were to be completed by the Borough Surveyor, one of whose assistants was the young Thomas Holte, later a photographer of many productions in the theatre. The Borough Council's River and Recreation Ground Committee approved the plans on 30 March, but put the garden scheme aside for future consideration as not all the site was yet available.[116] The Great Western Railway still owned land and disused warehouses near the tramway bridge.[117] The layout of the gardens scheme was much helped when the railway company agreed to sell some of this ground to the theatre Governors at a reduced price to allow the gardens to be developed.[118] The Borough Surveyor submitted his plan for the completion of the gardens on 28 September 1931 and it was approved by the Council's committee in October.[119] The garden plan also took into account the Corporation's intention that the tramway bridge be replaced by a new road bridge to allow ancient Clopton Bridge to be reserved as a tourist and footbridge only.[120] The remainder of the surroundings of the old canal basin was finally sold to the Stratford-upon-Avon Corporation in 1933.

CONSTRUCTION

The construction of the new Memorial Theatre began in 1928 with Holliday and Greenwood contracted to create the foundations. As with the first theatre, there were considerable difficulties with underground water on the site. The water problems, including the discovery of a stream flowing into the river from the north of the town, led to the appointment of B. L. Hurst as consulting engineer. It eventually took over £11,000 to ensure a stable, watertight foundation as excavations had to be made to a depth of 30 feet, 17 feet below the river bed level.[121] A concrete raft was formed over 340 piles and the internal surface was covered with asphalt to form a waterproof tank for the basement of the building.[122]

The Governors had discussed asking a member of the Royal Family to lay the foundation stone but delays over the site drainage precluded time for such a plan. The official laying of the foundation finally took place on 2 July 1929 with full Masonic honours, led by the Most Worshipful Pro-Grand Master, the Right Honourable Lord Ampthill. The foundation stone from

Edgehill, weighing over a ton, was placed in position after a time-capsule glass casket had been put into a specially-designed cavity in its base. The casket contained samples of all the coins of the realm, together with a copy of the latest issue of each of the *Daily Telegraph*, *The Times*, the *Birmingham Post* and the *Stratford-upon-Avon Herald*, and of the Royal Charter of the Shakespeare Memorial Theatre, accompanied by the official programme for the day.[123] Watched by over 600 freemasons and an enclosure full of people who had contributed to the rebuilding fund, Lord Ampthill was handed a silver trowel by the architect. (Elisabeth Scott was the first woman to have been allowed to participate in a Masonic ceremony of this kind.) Then an ancient Egyptian maul, or mallet, was used to dedicate the stone and its building

> *to be a house to commemorate the name of William Shakespeare and to promote that dramatic art of which he gave the greatest example to the world and to be a temple of concord and conciliation among the nations of the world.*[124]

Although the audience for the occasion included many prominent people, such as theatre personalities Sir Barry Jackson and Sir Frank Benson, there was understandable press comment querying why the ceremony was not carried out by, or at least with the aid of, actors whose professional home the new theatre would be.[125]

For months after the stone was laid there were further delays as more foundation work had to be completed, including the removal of a deep footing of the old canal basin that was discovered to be in the way. It was not until June 1930 that the firm of G. E. Wallis and Sons of Maidstone in Kent, with their craftsmen, took over the building of the theatre's superstructure, led by foreman E. G. Miller and Clerk of Works R. C. Long. Wallis's tender had been the lowest submitted for the work and quoted £127,000 for a project lasting seventy-eight weeks. This firm had previous experience of construction work on buildings in the public eye including the Royal Agricultural Hall, Westminster, and the Royal Academy of Music in London.[126]

One of the first tasks was to build the riverside terrace along the bank above the Avon. To do this, the river level had to be lowered at the weir below the parish church, and, to avoid interference with the daytime operation of the mill, the work was carried out at night. On 23 October

1930, as the men worked under floodlights, 6,000 bags of cement were lowered into the water to complete a wall that, when the river rose, would solidify into a terrace 134 feet long and 13 feet wide.[127]

Work then moved ahead well and within two years all was nearing completion. Comments on the building's appearance were to be found in the press up and down the country. 'Miss Scott has achieved a dramatic effect in the massing of the building', wrote A. E. Richardson in the *Builder.*[128] Archie Flower's letter to Harley Granville-Barker back in May 1928, had commented:

> *As for the external appearance, her definitely modern elevation has met with a wonderful approval in architectural circles ... ... It has been deemed by many individuals (including a lot of parsons) as like some medieval fortress ... ... whatever is built can never please everybody.*[129]

Plans were laid for a royal opening by the Prince of Wales on 23 April 1932, as the town celebrated Shakespeare's birthday. In honour of the occasion the flags of the nations were grouped around the theatre approaches in Waterside, instead of in their usual Bridge Street positions, and the unfurling was delayed until after the official luncheon had been held in a tent in New Place gardens, where speeches were made by Sir Frank Benson and the former Prime Minister, Stanley Baldwin. The Chairman, Archibald Flower, who had been knighted in the New Year honours in 1930, led William Bridges-Adams and Elisabeth Scott to meet Prince Edward.

The Prince's speech after he had unfurled the Union flag was heard by few in the crowd as there was a fault in the loud-speaker system, but for those who listened on the radio his message was clear as he praised the building before him.

> *Shakespeare himself would not have asked for another statue to be erected in his honour: he would have desired nothing better than that his plays should find a permanent home within a hundred yards of the church where he lies ... ... Nothing can more truly be called a memorial than such a theatre, which perpetuates, side by side with the historical memory of our greatest dramatist, the living spirit of his genius.*[130]

Elisabeth Scott then handed the Prince a large silver-gilt key, the door was ceremonially unlocked and the Prince and the audience went inside.

The afternoon's performance was *Henry IV, Part 1* presented by the loyal members of the Festival Company, who had moved from the temporary theatre in Greenhill Street back, at last, to the Memorial, led by Randle Ayrton and Fabia Drake. *Henry IV, Part 2* was staged in the evening, and now the public had their first sight of the interiors of the new theatre. During the intervals in the two plays they were able to look around them. Throughout the foyers, refreshment and bar areas as well as the auditorium, they found the very best of craftsmen's handiwork carried out in the finest of timbers from around the world, with modern metalwork, and both bold and subtle colouring in painted decoration. Details down to the built-in ashtrays and the cloakroom chairs had all been carefully included in the design concept.

F. R. S. Yorke was one of the first to write in detail about the immediate impact. 'Modern materials' he wrote in the *Architectural Review* 'are introduced not as a novelty, but for the performance of functions to which they are better suited than traditional ones.'[131] Although over the years changes have adapted the bars and refreshment room facilities, as well as the seating capacity and appearance of the auditorium, many of the original specialist features remain to be admired today.

A Tour in 1932

The theatre entrance facing the driveway was protected by a cantilevered marquise roof, or canopy, of overlapped aluminium, brass and copper. The visitor came into the foyer through the bold front doors made by George Parnall and Company. Directly ahead was the box office decorated in stainless steel, bronze and silver bronze to the designs of James Gibbons. To the left was an archway above which was mounted a bold but simple clockface, the mechanism of which was linked to the other clocks in the building so that all were synchronized. Beyond the arch lay one of the building's most attractive features, the flowing staircase of Swedish green marble, with Hornton stone steps and decorative brickwork in the adjacent wall, with bricks by Williamson and Cliff of Stamford. 'One of the glories of the building and a really remarkably fine piece of work', said the *Architect and Building News. (Pl. 7a)*

The staircase led up from a fountain court where the verdi de Prata marble centrepiece was surrounded by a pool with colourful vitreous mosaic incorporating the masks of Comedy and Tragedy in gold, reds and vivid blues. The fountain was designed by Gertrude Hermes[132] and was lit from above the stairwell where the far away star-shaped ceiling, painted in blue-grey and sea green, concealed spot-lights angled to the ground. The stair handrail, with its curves and angles, was another example of the 'outstanding use of metal decoration'.[133] *(Pl.9)*

Ascending the stairs to the dress circle, the mezzanine doors to the restaurant were the visitor's first encounter with the exquisite timberwork of John P. White and Sons of Pyghtle Works in Bedford. These doors of blistered mahogany had a delicate and detailed inlay decoration of ebony bands representing the tools used in the construction of the theatre building, from the architect's tee-square and tape to drain scrapers and hammers. Further up the stairs the cloaks vestibule was painted in deep vermilion and black with an ochre ceiling. This was the lobby beyond which lay the circle foyer with a bar counter at the far end made of English burr elm joinery and metalwork, decorated with Indian laurel, grey sycamore, ebony, rosewood and Honduras mahogany. *(Pl.8b, 13d)*

Curtains in the dress circle foyer were printed silk designed by John Armstrong,[134] and flanked full-length windows to the north side which overlooked the Bancroft gardens. An architectural critic remarked:

> *the fundamental reason for the charm of the room is to be found partly in the fenestration, the spacing and proportion of the windows seems exactly right, and partly in the subtle charming colour scheme which Mr Walpole Champneys has given it.*[135]

Walpole Champneys had experience in interior design of other public buildings, including the Regent cinema in Brighton, which had led to his commission to create the colour schemes for the new Memorial Theatre. Throughout the building he used his understanding of the effects of artificial light on fabrics and paintwork to produce colour schemes which ranged from bold to muted and subtle, according to the emphasis that the surroundings of each space required.

In the ground floor bar, leading off the fountain court, more of J. P. White's fine joinery, and swan-headed handles designed by Gertrude Hermes, were to be seen on the entrance doors. On the doors Indian silver-grey wood and sycamore were inlaid with aluminium alloy and ebony, while the bar counter had decoration in Indian silver-grey with irregular angle-cut lines and sunk Andaman padouk strips. 'A notable quality of all the decorative woodwork is the freshness and originality of the abstract patternwork. It is remarkably good, free from traditional taint, but very charming.'[136] Most of the original doors remain throughout the public areas of the theatre. The timber colour has matured but they are as pleasing today as sixty years ago.[137] *(Pl.8a, 13c)*

In 1932 the floors everywhere were also decorative. The entrance foyer was paved with contrasting stone, green from Hornton, brown from Ashburton and grey from Ancaster. In the dress circle lobby and the circular gallery bar, on the top floor above the main staircase, the floors were of inlaid cork which was to prove so durable that it was fifty years before it needed replacement. In the dress circle foyer a carpet first laid in the 1950s has protected the original floor which survives underneath. New materials were used such as in the ceiling designed by Mollo and Egan for the gallery bar, which was finished with plastic paint.[138] Ceiling detail elsewhere included cloud-shaped embossed patterns in the ground floor refreshment room. These were painted out in the 1950s but the feature was restored in the redecoration of 1978. Furniture was designed by Gordon Russell, of Broadway, for all the bars and the restaurant in 1932 and there were specially-designed metal lighting brackets for these rooms, of which those in the dress circle foyer survive.

> *The great interest in texture and colour of materials such as stones, woods and metals are made to produce their own decorative characteristics rather than relying on the conventions and shapes born on the drawing board. The design has arisen from the materials, not the materials chosen to suit the drawing ... ... The result is that the most insignificant fittings are both suited to their purpose and play their parts in a decorative ensemble.*

This judgement of the *Architect and Building News* is still valid when looking today at the doors, ceilings and staircases. The overall design effect, differing completely from the style of the previous generation, demonstrated Elisabeth Scott's claim in 1927 that she was a modernist.

The Auditorium

The most important public space in the theatre was the auditorium which had received very careful thought from all concerned in its design. T. C. Kemp noted that the first audiences admired its spaciousness and 'the chaste dignity of the colour schemes', while J. C. Trewin said that the room was 'a little alarming at first to playgoers brought up on plush and gilt.'[139]

To accommodate a thousand seats the auditorium was very gently fan-shaped with most seats facing almost directly forwards as in a cinema. This was in complete contrast to the wrap-around horseshoe arrangement that had been so admired by many in the old Memorial Theatre. The competition suggestion of two tiers above the stalls had been followed but the gallery at the top of the house was reached by a separate entrance with its own pay-desk and staircase on the street side of the main entrance. There were 494 seats in the stalls, with fifteen in row A widening to forty-five in row O at the back. In the dress circle 239 seats were staggered between thirty-two and thirty-seven in a row to give good sight lines. The gallery held a further 267 people on bench seating.

On either side of the front of the stage, emphasising the proscenium arch, were substantial brick portals faced in decorative Australian timber panelling. It was intended by Elisabeth Scott that these walls should always be a part of the stage scenery, while they also had a practical acoustic purpose. At the back of the dress circle was the only box that remained from the original plan. This Royal Box was dismantled after the opening performance when it had been occupied by the Prince of Wales, but the retiring room behind, which had telephone communication with back-stage, remained to be converted into observation rooms for the director and for the electrical control panels for the stage productions.[140] *(Pl.11a)*

The colour schemes for the auditorium were very carefully chosen by Champneys according to the competition's instructions that 'any decoration should direct the eye towards the stage'.[141] The main feature was a magnificent, top-lit, patchwork, artificial-silk velvet curtain hanging in front of the stage, with claret and black central panels radiating sideways and upwards through lighter shades to red, grey, rich yellows and white. The back wall of the stalls was of black woodwork with scarlet stanchions, but this soon had to be modified with fabric to assist acoustics. Decorative woodwork covered the walls of the dress circle, with horizontal veneers of Australian walnut, and inlays of ebony and rosewood. The proscenium arch was surmounted in grey sycamore with Andaman padouk strips across its width. The remainder of the walls, and the ceiling, were of oyster-blue. In artificial light, the impression was of an uncluttered richness, producing an overall effect of grey-blue highlighted by the woodwork, with silver and pale yellow and touches of crimson and vermilion. *(Pl.10a)*

The pairs of double doors at the back of the stalls had finger-plates of the masks of Comedy and Tragedy, designed by Gertrude Hermes and made by J. Gibbons. These were of superimposed sheets of aluminium alloy. This was unfortunately reflective and the plates had later to be removed as actors objected to the dazzle they created during performances.[142] Fingerplates, based on the original design, were restored in the auditorium refitting of 1988.

The padded seats, which were of modern rubber, instead of traditional springs and horsehair, had been specially designed by Sir Herbert Austin, of motor car fame. They featured arms that tipped up with the seats when they were not in use. The upholstery was in mohair of grey with a pattern of pink.[143] Soon the back of some of the stalls seats were adorned with plaques to honour those who had subscribed £1,000 or more towards the building. The patrons were invited to choose the name of a famous actor or theatre personality for a commemorative plate. Ellen Terry and David Garrick were chosen by Sir Archie and Lady Flower, while the Stratford-upon-Avon Borough Council selected the founder, Charles Edward Flower, and his wife for their seats. This practice of naming seats was revived in 1975 to help raise funds for the Centenary appeal towards the air-conditioning plant. Donors were asked for a minimum of £500 plus the cost of the plaque, and the practice continues today to mark special donations. Over the years, memorials have included the names of Dame Peggy Ashcroft, Trevor Nunn and many others of recent fame associated with the building.

Behind Champneys' drop curtain, a safety curtain had been hand-decorated by Vladimir Polunin, with the help of his wife. Polunin, who was Professor of Theatrical Design at the Slade school, executed a panel of delicate pastel colours showing a 10-foot high central figure of William Shakespeare, against the Warwickshire countryside. This was surrounded by a series of scenes from the plays.[144]

In the auditorium, as well as in the rest of the theatre, specially created lighting arrangements had been installed, with the help of the architect's lighting advisers, Harold Ridge and A. S. Aldred. Light sources were skilfully concealed in the ceiling of the auditorium, four ceiling-mounted spotlights covered the forestage, and eight further spotlights were hidden in front of the dress circle rails. Other facilities in the auditorium included air extraction vents in the ceiling for atmosphere control, which could give the auditorium a complete air change within one minute. Vacuum-cleaning extractors in the risers of the aisle floors were also neatly placed out of sight, and are still in use today.[145]

As the first audiences in the new Shakespeare Memorial Theatre relaxed in the river room, overlooking the grass-covered terrace beside the Avon, or sampled the menu in the small restaurant on the mezzanine floor, there was a general feeling of surprise and approval. The *Shakespeare Pictorial* in July of the opening year suggested that intervals should be extended from ten to thirty minutes to allow patrons to appreciate their surroundings. The building had a feeling of luxury and elegance, fulfilling the hopes and dreams of its Chairman. The *Architect and Building News* said the theatre had

> *a freshness of thought brought to bear on its design from the general conception down to the smallest details. While it is as efficient a vehicle for the presentation of plays as the resources of modern theatre design and construction can make it, as a work of architecture it reveals that no less thought and time have been expended on small details than on greater matters, a thing all too rare in modern building.*

The exterior of the building excited much journalistic comment and the *Birmingham Post* in August 1931 had been most outspoken against the use of red brick in so solid a construction. The theatre was strongly defended in a resulting correspondence and Elisabeth Scott was congratulated for 'a rest from the threat of half-timber'.[146] The designer of much of the theatre's interior furniture, Gordon Russell, also defended the new theatre which elsewhere was called a 'jam-factory' and a 'crematorium'. The correspondent of the *Lady* saw it as natural that many people were puzzled by 'the purposeful brick towers of Miss Scott's serene building', but firmly stated that this was 'the best modern theatre that can be devised and incidentally provides also a memorial of the taste and ability of our own time.'[147]

Although many cinemas were built between the wars, which often showed exuberant use of colour and decoration in their interior designs, there were few new theatres in Britain from which Chesterton, Shepherd and Scott could derive ideas. Two theatres of similar size to the Shakespeare Memorial, the Cambridge and the Phoenix, had opened in London in 1930, and Sir Giles Gilbert Scott, second cousin of Stratford's architect, had worked on the Phoenix with Bertie Crew and Cecil Massey, with advice from Theodore Komisarjevsky. A similar lively use of colour and materials had featured in both these buildings. The difficulty for the Stratford architects lay in achieving suitable facilities for the stage and in the practical working areas beyond.[148]

The Stage in 1932

Before the competition was launched in 1927 the Festival Director, William Bridges-Adams, had drawn up specifications of what was required for both the stage and the auditorium. However, Archie Flower and the adjudicators had not wanted to inhibit the competitors in their ideas and the guidelines had been simplified. Instead of the horse-shoe shaped seating plan requested by the director, the chosen auditorium had no side boxes and was unsuited to close contact between the actor and his audience. Bridges-Adams was to write many years later that they had built 'the theatre, of all theatres in England, in which it is hardest to make an audience laugh or cry.'[149]

Bridges-Adams had been adamant that a proscenium arch was required. This was built 21 feet high and 30 feet wide and it was integral with its fly tower so that it later proved to be virtually impossible to achieve a flexibility beyond the 'picture-frame' performance area. In front of the proscenium was a 17 foot deep forestage between the enclosing timber-fronted walls that concealed assembly areas on either side. Part of the forestage could be removed to reveal steps leading down under the stage, or an orchestra pit was created if all the downstage 12 foot section was taken out.

Behind the proscenium Elisabeth Scott, Maurice Chesterton and their advisers, Knight and Company, the engineers for stage equipment, had installed some of the most modern technical apparatus including two rolling stages each of 38 by 15 feet. This was the first rolling stage installed in England and was intended to allow swift scene changes by silently gliding each set into position from the side. The design followed European prototypes and was chosen in preference to a revolving stage as it was believed to allow a quicker changeover and a more flexible staging area. In reality it meant that all scenery was placed well behind the proscenium arch, and the wide forestage became an undesirable gulf isolating the actors from their audience. Also, due to a lack of width on the site, the extension sides of the rolling stages had been so positioned that it was not possible to erect a whole set in the wings thereby defeating much of the purpose of this equipment.[150]

There were two bridges, or lifts, each 33 feet across the width of the stage. The downstage lift was 9 feet deep while the upstage one spanned 6 feet. Their use was limited, however, by the sightlines from the gallery as the proscenium cut off the view of the rear lift if it was in its raised position, 8 feet above the stage. The lifts could descend 16 feet below the stage floor but this was not deep enough to allow tall scenery to be fully lowered out of view. As the lifts were built below the rolling stages individual productions had to use either, but not both stage floor variations. The rolling stage sections that crossed the main stage, over the lifts, were finally dismantled in the 1940s, although in the wings their location may still be seen in the floor grooves, and a remnant of the wall-mounted section remains. The lifts are still in position and have been used occasionally in recent years, most notably in 1991 for the spectacular Battle of Shrewsbury tableau in *Henry IV, Part 1*.[151]

The requirement for a large stage had been met in Elisabeth Scott's design and the fly-tower above was, generally, quite adequate for the storage and flying of scenery needed in the constantly changing day-to-day repertoire of the Shakespeare seasons.[152] The stage was 45 feet deep and the height to the grid was 65 feet above the stage floor. At the rear of the stage was a huge plaster cyclorama, suspended on a metal frame. It weighed 22 tons yet a simple pulley system allowed the wall to move downstage as far as the rear lift when required. Top lighting allowed almost any colour to play on the plaster and concealed lamps could provide a star or cloud effect for the back of a stage set without the need for painted back cloths. For more traditional designers a paint frame and gallery hung at the rear of the stage, but its use had ceased by the mid-1970s and it was finally removed in 1991.

Behind the stage the facilities were soon found to be less than satisfactory. The dressing rooms were on three floors all along the street side of the theatre, but they were narrow and cramped. While each two-actor room had a shower and a bath of hip-bath proportions, there was insufficient space to hang costumes ready for use. The dressing-room windows looked out onto the area where the sometimes noisy gallery patrons eagerly queued on their stools beside the balcony door: for access to their separate box office and seats was not opened until shortly before each performance.

Despite Bridges-Adams' urgent request, there was no green-room or leisure area which actors could use for relaxation, although the public refreshment rooms were good for their immediate purposes. Only two small administration offices had been included, and the small rehearsal room was soon taken over for other uses. Below the rake of the dress circle Miss Scott had built a mezzanine for wardrobe and costume storage, and a carpenters' space lay behind the stage, with an outside entrance onto a small parking area for deliveries or emergency vehicle use.[153] Musicians' rooms were squeezed into the basement, on the street side, from where the players could pass directly down a corridor to the orchestra pit. As in many theatres of the time there was no front-of-house access for staff to pass backstage without going across the stage or out-of-doors.

Controversy about the building and its efficiency has persisted over the years. What in 1927 had seemed to both the architect and producers to be an ideal playing space was out of date within ten years. Sixty years later Iain Mackintosh summed up the situation:

> *The lesson of Stratford-upon-Avon's story is twofold: firstly that, despite the fact that the client did say clearly what he wanted, he did not get it although he thought all was well until the opening night; secondly that the architect thought she had created what she had not: a focused intimate theatre. The theatre profession, when roused, is more vociferous than the architectural profession and the nation accepted the theatrical view: it was all the fault of the architect. It is clear that there had been a breakdown in communication between the two professions.*[154]

Elisabeth Scott stuck by her concept, however, when she wrote to the *Daily Telegraph* on 30 September 1943 to say that in her view it was the limited approaches of the producers (or, as we would call them today, directors) rather than the fault of the theatre itself that caused so much dissent and adverse criticism.

'However,' as T. C. Kemp later wrote, 'there the building was: impressive, solid and immovable, and the company settled down to the task of playing in it.'[155] In 1929 Archie Flower had stated that there was £250,000 available for the theatre and an endowment,[156] and the theatre's annual report of 1934 stated that the whole building had cost £192,000 of which half had been paid for by the American Shakespeare Foundation. The Royal Insurance Company had paid £25,000 in May 1926 as compensation after the fire. In its new Memorial Theatre the Company, still under the leadership of William Bridges-Adams, set out to fulfil public expectations. 'The world had decided that Stratford must be to Shakespeare what Bayreuth is to Wagner, and Salzburg to Mozart, and it was not for Stratford to say no.'[157]

Completing the Project

Once the theatre was open and in operation the next task was to tidy up the ruined site of the old theatre. From 1926 until 1932 the only work that had been carried out here was to remove the dangerous remains of twisted roof girders and to lay a solid concrete floor. From the time of the architects' competition onwards there had been plans to convert the site of the old theatre into a much-needed conference hall for the use of the townspeople.[158] Before the new theatre was complete *The Times*[159] had referred to the Victorian library and art gallery wing as an 'excrescence' that should be replaced by a library more in keeping with the new building. The library and gallery had miraculously escaped all damage from the fire and their contents had been saved; but the collections no longer had the importance for the theatre's Governors that had been placed on them by the founder. The surviving building and its contents were considered worth retaining as a place of research and of tourist interest but its existence did not impinge on the real work of the theatre. The Governors felt the collection could not merit major expenditure on administration or upkeep. The building would be simply refurbished, but no more.

In December 1931 the Chairman, Sir Archibald Flower, had announced that the architectural team of Scott, Chesterton and Shepherd would prepare plans for conversion of the shell of the old theatre into a conference hall, once their work on the new theatre was complete.[160] The following

November the plans were revealed for a hall to seat 400, with a small platform, an exhibition gallery and committee rooms, as well as storage space for theatre scenery as the theatre's backstage areas were already proving inadequate. A flat asphalted roof within the walls of the old theatre would enclose the space.[161]

The building of the Conference Hall was carried out by G. E. Wallis and Sons in recognition of their excellent work on the new theatre. Little of the surviving exterior of the old Memorial was changed. New exit doors were created through the unusually thick walls leading out into Elisabeth Scott's riverside loggia, and curved staircases at the south end of the hall concealed the committee rooms, one on each side of the original theatre door into the garden. The main hall was approached through a vestibule leading off the old carriageway entrance to the first theatre. The brickwork of the interior was covered with natural-coloured acoustic wall-boards under the direction of Hope Bagenal who had been acoustic adviser to the architects for the new Memorial Theatre. Tip-up removable seating was provided by Bennett Furnishing Company, set out on a floor of gurjun wood which was intended to serve also as a dance floor as occasion demanded. Another of the old team, Walpole Champneys, advised Miss Scott on the decoration, and long curtains were designed to hang from the ceiling behind the small curved exhibition balcony on the south wall.[162] Natural lighting was achieved by the use of clerestory windows above the suspended ceiling of the main hall. *(Pl.15a)*

On 15 July 1933 the new Conference Hall, which had cost the Governors £10,000, was opened by Lady Constance Benson. With her husband, Sir Frank, she had led the acting company at Stratford for many years in the old Memorial Theatre and, as she said in her remarks at the opening ceremony, they would always remember the building as 'the little theatre'. The first event in the new hall, which followed Lady Benson's speech, was the inaugural meeting of the Warwickshire branch of the English Folk Dance and Song Society, with displays of morris, country and sword dancing. Thereafter the Conference Hall was in regular use and small modifications were made from time to time to improve its comfort and facilities.

While work went ahead on construction of the Conference Hall in 1932-33, the Bancroft gardens on the bridge side of the theatre were completed at a cost to the Borough Council of £10,000. The last of the old, disused warehouses disappeared and three-and-a-half acres of lawns were laid out with some preserved and other newly-planted chestnut trees. The old canal basin became 'a sheet of ornamental water', and boats did not reappear there until 11 July 1964 when a festival was held in the Bancroft basin to commemorate the re-opening of the Stratford to Birmingham canal for tourist traffic.[163]

The final act of the creation of this riverside park was the removal of the Gower Monument from behind the old theatre where Shakespeare's statue had faced towards the church, to a new position beside the pool from where the statue looked out over the Warwickshire countryside to the north. The re-siting was completed in June 1933 but, on 22 June 1946, the theatre Governors minuted a request they wished to make to the Borough Council that Shakespeare's statue should be turned to face the theatre. There is no record, however, that the suggestion was ever formally received or discussed.[164] The statue remains on its 1933 site and, since the building of Bridgeway and the Hilton Hotel (now the Moat House) in the early 1970s, the statue has watched over the thousands of tourists who stream into the town on Shakespeare's account each year.[165]

The Bancroft gardens layout was little changed until the mid-1980s when the District Council created a large stone-edged flower-bed immediately in front of the theatre, upsetting the intention of the garden design conceived in the 1930s to place the emphasis on the theatre's facade, just as, within, the eye was drawn towards the stage. The theatre's own gardens to the south of the building were improved over the years and from 1947 until the late 1970s the beds were tended by the gardeners of the Shakespeare Birthplace Trust.

Avonbank house had become the parish vicarage after the death of Sarah Flower, but its fabric needed much attention. Other uses were considered but the house was eventually demolished in 1956 (at a cost of £1,010). The garden house or orangery which included stone from the former College, in Mill Lane, was repaired by the theatre's maintenance staff to become a garden store and the site became a pleasant tree-lined garden. The sloping lawns, next to the churchyard, beyond Avonbank's ornamental garden wall were laid out as an area for an open-air theatre for visiting university theatre groups.[166] The lawns became the Centenary green garden in 1975, when plots, each a foot square, were leased out to help raise money for the new air-conditioning in the theatre. This garden was inaugurated by Her Majesty Queen Elizabeth II in brilliant sunshine on Friday 27 June 1975 and for a year a statue on loan from Henry Moore was on display here.

The attractions of the riverside restaurant facilities were such that ideas to extend the premises were discussed as early as 1935. The architects advised that, if the terrace restaurant was to be altered, the appearance of the building from the riverside would be improved if the dining room on the first floor was also extended. To begin with, when the gallery seating was extended in 1936, a refreshment room was also created overlooking the river above the flat roof of the restaurant and kitchens. The following year plans were drawn up for an extension over the sloping grass terrace, to give a long, narrow tearoom on the ground floor and corresponding restaurant space above. Elisabeth Scott, now in partnership with John C. Shepherd and John Breakwell,[167] designed the rooms so that few changes were needed to the existing service rooms and kitchens, but added small washroom facilities at mezzanine level on a new staircase connecting the ground and first floors. The alterations were carried out in the early months of 1938 and supplied additional seating for 200 with little interior modification beyond the simple device of using existing window openings to create access points to the new rooms.

Many of the old team were brought together once more as builders G. E. Wallis and Sons set about the task of cantilevering out over the river bank so that a 10 foot wide terrace remained beyond the windows. Crittalls, whose expertise in modern window design had been an admired feature of the theatre, designed metal french windows which were painted pale yellow with white frame bars. The columns supporting a narrow restaurant terrace above, were dark blue and pale green while the paint on the balcony soffits was Venetian red. The railings along the river edge, made by Parker, Winder and Achurch, were pale blue above silver grey teak weather boarding. The terraces were completed with flower boxes of Canadian cedar. *(Pl.6b)*

Indoors the restaurant decor had modern plastic paint on the walls, finished with twirled brush strokes, and colourful abstract curtain wall-hangings designed by Walpole Champneys and made by the Disabled Sailors and Soldiers Mutual Association. Globe light fittings were linked by decorative metalwork by Ascog Limited and hung above Gordon Russell's wooden tables and chairs. Instead of the wood floors elsewhere in the theatre, floor surfaces were to be of non-slip cellulin, a material used successfully on the Queen Mary liner.[168] It was the completion of the terraces and restaurants that finally gave the theatre a less stark external

9. Fountain court and staircase: *a)* 1932.

b) 1971.

10. Auditorium view towards stage
a) 1932.

b) 1962 (*Midsummer Night's Dream* set)

c) 1993. (*King Lear* set)

11. a) Auditorium, view from the stage 1932.

b) View from the stage 1974 (Set for *Measure for Measure*)
(Note side balcony and slips.)

12. Shakespeare Memorial Theatre, from the north, 1947. (Note: Eric Kennington sculptures above dress circle foyer windows, and scenery store building of 1889 at extreme right.) Inset: Kennington sculpture 'Treachery'.

appearance and was to earn the building the description of looking at night like an ocean liner moored at the side of the Avon.[169]

Apart from periodic redecoration and refurbishment, the restaurant's public areas changed little until the lower windows were moved outwards in 1978. They are now flush with the overhang of the restaurant floor above, and only a narrow terrace remains overlooking the river. The dining room seating capacity was reduced in 1966 to allow for a higher standard of meals to be offered.[170] The two refreshment rooms were called the Bankside Restaurant and the River Room until the names Box Tree Restaurant above, with the River Terrace for the buffet below, were introduced in 1981. This was after only a year when the upper facilities were divided into the Bankside Square Bistro and the Terrace Restaurant, above the River Room.

The Auditorium: change and development

The number of cheaper seats in the theatre was proved to be inadequate in 1935 when an exceptionally fine summer and the lowering of admission prices due to the exemption of theatres from entertainment tax combined to bring record crowds to Stratford-upon-Avon. The following winter alterations were made by Theatre Equipment Limited of Wardour Street, London, to add 150 more bench seats at the back of the gallery.[171]

The auditorium continued to be a source of actors' distress and audience disquiet throughout the 1930s. The distance between the proscenium arch and the front stalls, and difficulties of hearing from some areas of the stalls when actors faced upstage from a mid-stage position were continual sources of complaint. In September 1943 the actor Baliol Holloway defended his colleagues against charges of inaudibility in a letter to the *Daily Telegraph*.[172] Alterations were carried out first in 1944 and again in 1948.

Robert Atkins came to Stratford as director of the theatre festivals in the last year of the war but before he signed his contract he insisted that some internal changes must be made to help achieve a closer actor-audience relationship. The root of the problem lay in what Richard Leacroft was later to describe as 'a standard picture-frame theatre with a cyclorama.'[173] The proper use of the fore-stage could not be made if the bridges, rolling stages and upstage areas were the focus for action and scenery. The resulting gulf led to audience alienation. Even in the 1990s some acoustic problem remains and an actor standing mid-stage behind the proscenium cannot easily be heard in some parts of the stalls, particularly directly below the overhang of the front of the dress circle.

Attempts in 1944 to try to resolve the situation led to the covering of the orchestra pit and the steps down into it with a floor that was level with the main stage. At the same time new spotlights were installed to bring more light to the fore-stage as Atkins believed that if the audience could see better their hearing might also 'improve'.[174] These alterations benefited the coming season but full redecoration and refurbishment of the theatre was deferred until Sir Barry Jackson took over as Festival Director at the end of the war. The first major overhaul of stage machinery since the theatre opened was carried out in 1946 under the guidance of Hoare, Lea and Partners, at a cost of £2,950, with Frank Ballard, chief-machinist of the Royal Opera House, Covent Garden as adviser.[175]

A further extensive scheme of alterations was undertaken after Anthony Quayle became Festival Director in 1950. The Champneys drop curtain had already been replaced by red velvet in 1949 and in the 1949-50 season temporary balconies, draped in black, were erected either side of the proscenium arch, for musicians; but the new Chairman of the theatre Governors, Sir Archie's son, Fordham Flower, was in full agreement with his new director that radical changes were needed to bring the theatre up-to-date. Quayle wrote in his autobiography:

> *The building was of a hideousness that nobody who had not sat in it could possible appreciate. It was built like a cinema, a long shoe-box of a place. The walls were lined with big panels of french-polished wood ... ... these panels were not only garish to look at but light bounced off them during the action of the play. The dress circle was set so far back that you were almost sitting outside the theatre. It was a monstrosity ... ... One of the first jobs that I was obliged to do was to pull the dress circle nearer to the stage, thrust two wings out on either side so that the dress circle audience was linked visually and physically with the action, and tear down the dreadful strips of shiny veneer.*[176]

So in the course of time views of Elisabeth Scott's lovingly-completed audience hall had changed. Over £80,000 was spent in the winter of 1950-51 as Quayle's alterations were put into effect. The scheme was planned and overseen by architect Brian O'Rorke who was chiefly known for his interior designs for ocean liners. Since 1946 he had been working as architect, in succession to Sir Edwin Lutyens, on the National Theatre to be built in London.[177]

For the Memorial Theatre's auditorium O'Rorke reshaped the rake of the seating, restepping the floor to allow two more rows of seats to be built at the rear of the stalls. The circle was extended forward, adding a row of seats at the front, and three single row boxes were built at dress circle level along each of the side walls. In all 135 more seats were accommodated. The capacity was now 1,377, with 565 in the stalls, 326 in the circle, and 450 in the balcony, with standing room for 76.[178] To achieve the additional space new seats, designed by Maples of London, each two inches narrower than those of Herbert Austin, were installed. The name-plaques on the backs sponsored by theatre patrons were transferred to the new seating when the work was complete.[179] *(Pl.10b)*

The whole theatre colour scheme was changed at this time and the young designer Tibor Reich was commissioned to create new fabrics to be woven on his looms at Clifford Chambers.[180] For the auditorium seats Reich used his 'Tibor' trademarked 'Cardinal' fabric in burgundy red. A scarlet wool cloth was used for the backs of these seats, to create a two-tone look, reinforced by a new, bold red carpet. The 'Cardinal' cotton bouclé was used in forest green for the couches in the dress circle foyer. The 'theatre' colour schemes of red and gold so favoured by the Victorians, and frowned on in the 1930s, were creeping back into fashion as wall paint of dark mushroom pink replaced the variety of tones of Champneys' designs.[181] Nevertheless the new colour schemes were the height of 1950s 'post-war' style.

Tibor Reich also designed 'Macbeth' hand-woven cotton bouclé in scarlet on a dusty grey ground, with non-tarnishing gold thread, for new seating in the main bars, with 'Park Lane' deep burgundy red with a fleck of purple for the balcony bar, which had a carpet of the same colours. A chartreuse green with gold threads was used for the window curtains of the dress circle foyer and a striped 'Regency' fabric in mustard yellow and off-white on a dusty-pink ground framed the windows of the restaurant.

New light fittings were installed as part of a complete refit of the electrical scheme in the building. The old retiring room behind the Royal Box space was converted to accommodate stage lighting control equipment of the very latest design. From here seventy-four spotlights and seventy-two stage lighting circuits were to be controlled by an electrical valve system. With the final removal of the timber-fronted bastion assembly walls each side of the stage the forestage width was now 46 feet, 16 feet wider than in 1932, making it more difficult for designers to find a centre of focus for their settings.

Backstage, and visible to everyone who saw the theatre from the riverside, even more extensive improvements were made during the winter of 1950-51. The loggia, which had been built to screen the ruin of the old theatre and was now redundant as an interval bar area for the Conference Hall, was demolished and replaced by a new block designed by O'Rorke to create an actors' green room at ground floor level. This kind of social amenity space had been of importance in theatres since the eighteenth century, but sadly had been omitted in Elisabeth Scott's plans. If Stratford's theatre was to attract more star performers this facility was essential. In building the green room the foundation stone of the first Memorial Theatre was hidden by the construction of a storage cupboard, behind the servery counter, where it remains today.

Above the green room sixteen new dressing rooms were built to allow the existing rooms overlooking Waterside to be taken over as much-needed additional administration offices. The whole alteration scheme was overseen in the Company's absence during the winter months by Patrick Donnell, the theatre's stage director. The auditorium refit was ready for the opening of the 1951 Festival of Britain season in which the young Richard Burton starred in the *Henry IV* plays, *Henry V*, and *The Tempest*, while the green room and dressing room block was finished later in the season.[182] The final cost of the alterations was £21,120. Although they were planned in 1950-51, it was not until 1954 that four further dressing rooms (numbers 9-12) were built, above a Waterside general office entrance created when the stage door was moved to the rear of the stage.[183]

From time to time over the following years other alterations have been carried out, gradually softening the originally stark outline of the Scott building. From 1956 to 1986 the theatre's architect was Robert Harvey of Yorke, Harper and Harvey, of Cook's Alley, Stratford, and of Birmingham. In these years Harvey prepared plans for all the changes that were made and for others which were not implemented, usually for lack of funds. In

1958 a glazed outer foyer was built for the theatre below Elisabeth Scott's projecting roof of overlapping metals. The glass and metal doors designed by Harvey with silver-bronze handles were completed by Mr. Symon of the Birmingham architectural engineers, Henry Hope. This new entrance lobby had a few bench seats where patrons could await friends. It also gave better protection to the main foyer from inclement weather. The matching canopy that had provided rain cover for generations of gallery queues on the Waterside elevation had suffered more from deterioration, and after consultation with Brian O'Rorke, it had been temporarily repaired in 1955.[184] It was finally removed during the 1958 improvements.

The foyer alterations were completed at a cost of £7,600 by the Warwickshire firm of William Sapcote and Sons in February 1959. Later in the year the box office was enlarged by bringing it out further into the inner foyer. A small door was added so that access was no longer through the auditorium, which had frequently been inconvenient. The public appearance of the box office was little changed as the metal walls and ornamental grilles, or guichets, of the original design were retained.

Successive Festival Directors, or Artistic Directors as they have been known since the Royal Shakespeare Company was founded by Peter Hall in 1961, have each chosen to change the shape of the front of the stage of what was now re-named the Royal Shakespeare Theatre. When he was appointed in 1958 to succeed Glen Byam Shaw in 1960, Peter Hall said his dream was that Stratford and its theatre would 'prosper so that they will be able to pull down this theatre and build a new one which I as a director would be very happy to work in.'[185]

One of Peter Hall's first actions when he assumed the directorship of the theatre, was to ask Sean Kenny, the architect and stage designer, to draw up ideas for alterations to the auditorium and stage. Hall wanted to remove the proscenium arch and open up the stage into the wings at the same time as increasing the capacity of the audience to 2,000 in an amphitheatre around an apron stage, with a flying-grid over the forestage. Hall and Kenny felt 'this type of stage is essential if Shakespeare is to be produced properly ... ... the plays have been boxed in for too long.'[186] The Governors envisaged that the cost of such a major change would be in the region of £500,000 and the work would take up to six months to carry out.

It was quickly realised, however, that the proscenium arch could not be removed without the probability of the fly-tower's collapse. The project was dropped, and instead the front stalls seating was re-arranged to a plan drawn up by Peter Hall and stage designer Henry Bardon, with a projecting hexagonal forestage and a stage rake of one in eighteen. The alterations cost £8,228[187] and brought the stage as far forward as was possible without ruining sight-lines from the dress circle and balcony. Like all theatrical changes of fashion, this new presentation was deemed to be outdated within a few years. A revolving stage was introduced in 1960, when the cyclorama was finally removed, and this in turn was taken out in 1963 when a false proscenium was created, painted black, with the intention of drawing the audience's eyes towards a focal point at the centre of the stage which, for the *Wars of the Roses* (1963-64) was to be the throne of England.[188]

The final attempt at creating a horse-shoe style auditorium took place in 1972-73 when side-balcony seats and two rows of semi-standing positions were added along the walls at balcony level. These slips were devised by stage designer Christopher Morley, and built by engineers Ove Arup by cantilevering out from the 22 inch thick auditorium walls. Trevor Nunn's *Romans* season in 1972 required hydraulically-powered rising and tilting stage sections installed by Vickers of Swindon. Despite the great expense of this equipment it was seldom used after its first year and was completely removed in the early 1980s, although the hydraulic power supply continued to be useful.[189] *(Pl.11b)*

A major refit of the auditorium and the installation of modern air-conditioning was planned in detail during 1968 and 1969 but, as this would entail a very large capital expenditure, the major part of the work was deferred. The auditorium was nevertheless completely reseated in a warm orange and carpeted in a rich peacock-blue and grey stripe. This project was carried out by leading interior designers, Hille. At the same time the stalls and the adjacent bar were painted dark brown and black with mushroom walls for the circle and above. The red leather seats of the balcony were stained black.

Later, in 1976, the whole auditorium became dark chocolate-brown as a background to the natural timber stage-set for the season. The timbering continued round the front of the circle to create a wooden O and when the set changed the following year the timber facings on the balcony and circle fronts were painted to match the dark walls. As part of the 1968 refurbishment Christopher Morley was responsible for a re-presentation scheme for the main foyer which included the mounting of very large display photographs in V-shaped pairs high on the entrance walls, and new discreet lighting replaced the 1930s glass prism lights.

In 1968 the promise of an Arts Council grant of twenty per cent of the cost of the proposed alterations, and the planned sale of Avoncliffe, at Alveston (which had been the proposed site for a drama school in the 1930s, and was later home for Peter Hall), led to money eventually being available to launch what became the centenary appeal of 1975. The installation of air-conditioning and the conversion of the theatre to gas-fired heating was finally carried out a cost of £150,000 in the early months of 1976, under the supervision of Hoare, Lea and Partners of Birmingham, who had been heating engineering advisers to the theatre since the 1940s.[190]

In the 1980s and into the 1990s a very wide range of design requirements has been demanded of the stage that Bridges-Adams had wanted to be entirely flexible but which he had found to be restrictive. Raked stage floors have been slight or steep,[191] steps and various trapdoors have covered the stage but the old lifts remain *in situ* and can be exploited if designers are willing to study the theatre and its possibilities before embarking on work for a particular production. Modern technology has been applied to lighting and sound operation through the introduction of computers, but these are still operated from the old royal box position behind the dress circle. The Deputy Stage Manager's prompt corner is now usually a curtained-off area at the end of the side circle, stage left, from where microphone and closed circuit television communication can be kept with backstage throughout every performance.

Individual seasons have also seen alterations to the audience configuration, particularly for the 1976 season when the timbered balcony set allowed two tiers of seats on stage behind the acting area. In 1986-87 a few rows of bench seats were installed on the forestage, immediately in front of the proscenium arch,[192] and for 1988 stage designer, Bob Crowley, created seating below the dress circle which came down to the forestage on either side. The stalls sight-lines were badly affected by this arrangement and the new seating was removed the following winter.

In recent times a greater respect has been shown for the architectural heritage of Elisabeth Scott's building, so much so that in the spring of 1988 the front of the dress circle and the balcony were lowered to allow steel safety rails of 1930s style to be installed. At the same time art-deco design light fittings were placed around the auditorium. The black leather of 1969 was removed from the side doors into the auditorium and the 1930s veneers were revealed and restored to their former glory. New finger plates based on the original Hermes designs were made for the back auditorium doors. In 1993 the same style of steel rails has been installed at the front of the side circle and the balcony slips to complete the work begun in 1988. The total audience capacity after the 1993 refurbishment became 1500, with 656 in the stalls, 347 in the circle and 499 in the balcony. *(Pl.10c)*

Bars and Restaurants

The restaurant facilities of the theatre have always been recognised by the management as an important amenity for those members of the audience who regard a meal or a social drink as an integral part of a theatre visit. Over the years the facilities of the Royal Shakespeare Theatre have needed updating and modernisation to suit audience expectations and to meet improved health and safety standards. Despite this the basic spaces remain the same as those provided by Elisabeth Scott in her extensions completed in 1938.

The restaurant had a staircase, designed by Robert Harvey, added in 1977 to allow direct access from the river terrace when the theatre is closed, or when performances are in progress; and between 1971 and 1978 the windows overlooking the river were replaced in three stages, beginning at balcony level. The metal framed Crittall windows of 1936-38 were removed and plate-glass, double-glazed units in black anodised aluminium were installed to improve both the view and the insulation for the comfort of patrons. The final change here was in 1983, when the River Terrace Restaurant on the ground floor was extended with new plate glass windows to allow extra seating space beyond the pillars, retaining the clerestory of the 1938 extension.[193]

New carpets have been laid in the restaurants and bars and the rooms have been redecorated from time to time. Between 1974 and 1978 the bars had their colour schemes altered to chocolate and woodsmoke and the dress circle foyer furniture was replaced with modern cane and basket chairs. The original Gordon Russell sofas were re-covered to fit in with the woodsmoke colour scheme. The most recent change, in 1991, was in the River Terrace with art deco details, designed by Sue Ferguson, in deep green, musk pink and cream, after the 1970s browns had given way, from 1989, to a repainting programme of deep blue and cream.

In 1990 the stalls doors from the foyer had their crimson velvet curtains from the 1950s replaced on the recommendation of the company's graphic designer, Ginny Crow, who was put in charge of a front-of-house refurbishment. The chosen fabric was dark blue, red and green, reminiscent of Walpole Champneys' design schemes. This renewal programme was completed in the winter of 1991-92 when the dress circle bar was redesigned by Michael Reardon and Tim Furby, returning to the style of the 1930s, and a new coffee servery was installed in the former cloaks space at the head of the stairs. At the same time new arrangements were made for the shop in the main foyer to allow for more stock to be displayed on self-service shelves which could be enclosed in an elegant cupboard frontage out of opening hours. The shop was surmounted by a large RSC swan logo to face the clock at the far end of the foyer.

Over the years a variety of decorative features and memorials have been added to the foyers. A stone memorial, carved by Sir Robert Bird, was unveiled by Lord Iliffe in a position adjacent to the box office on 23 April 1953. This commemorated the years of devotion given to the theatre by the late Chairman, Sir Archie Flower. Above the memorial was placed the portrait of Charles Edward Flower painted by Phil R. Morris, A.R.A.. In June 1953 the Governors purchased a Mortlake tapestry of David Garrick as Richard III to be hung on the curved wall near the fountain, where it remained for a number of years. Other memorials beside the fountain include one completed in June 1963 to the American actor James K. Hackett who had left the substantial sum of $68,000 to the Shakespeare Memorial. A bronze tablet dedicated to American subscribers to the 1920s rebuilding and endowment fund, who later served with the Allies in the War, was also moved here from its first position in the main foyer.[194]

The Picture Gallery and Library

In the years following the fire that destroyed the first Memorial Theatre, the library and art gallery were refurbished, and Alfred Wareing, formerly manager at the Huddersfield Theatre Royal, was employed as librarian, with time allowed for writing, lecturing and arranging tours of the theatre. The pictures were returned to the gallery and their rehanging was organised by Sir Whitworth Wallace, Keeper of the Birmingham Art Gallery, so that the walls were not so crowded as before and each painting could be more clearly seen by visitors. Otherwise there were few alterations in the Victorian part of the theatre as attention focused on the new theatre and its first seasons. The library at this time came under the overall guidance of F. C. Wellstood, Secretary and Librarian of the Shakespeare Birthplace Trust, and for a year between 1938 and September 1939 the young Stratfordian, Paul Morgan, newly qualified as a librarian, was employed at the theatre.[195]

The emergency repairs required to all parts of the building complex immediately after the War led to the closure of the Picture Gallery in 1946 for redecoration and attention to damp problems. The library was also closed on the advice of its new Librarian, Levi Fox, who had recently come to Stratford as Wellstood's successor at the Shakespeare Birthplace Trust. A complete overhaul and rearrangement of the library was considered necessary to re-instate the collection as a research centre of international interest. An Assistant Librarian was appointed and the room that had previously served both as a museum and as the Librarian's office became a bookstack. The former book store room was turned into a reading room, while previous secretarial space became a staff office.

The growth of the Memorial Library and its archive led by 1956 to the theatre Governors' decision that the collection should be amalgamated with that of the Shakespeare Birthplace Trust to form a major centre for Shakespeare and theatre studies. In 1955 Avonbank had been considered as a possible home for the new research library[196] but, when this was seen to be unsuitable, it was agreed in principle to move the theatre library to Henley Street, into the former home of the Director of the Trust. On investigation this Victorian house also proved inadequate and so it was demolished to make way for the Shakespeare Centre to be built. The theatre's library move finally took place in the spring of 1964 when the new research centre opened next door to Shakespeare's Birthplace. The rooms at the theatre vacated by the library were used first as the Royal Shakespeare Company's membership mailing office, and later to house the first computers installed to assist the financial administration. Some of the library bookshelves were removed to the rare book business of former theatre manager, Robert Vaughan,[197] but the original heavy oak chairs and tables remain in the old library reading room which is now used by the RSC Collection and serves as a drinks room for the Swan Theatre intervals. Near the fireplace here, there also remains a memorial stone to Helen Faucit which was rejected by the nearby Holy Trinity church. The stone is much more appropriately placed in the building where this famous actress was the first leading lady, and to which her husband, Sir Theodore Martin, bequeathed a large number of books.

The Picture Gallery continued in its old premises although re-arrangements have been carried out over the years. The major alterations to the theatre in 1951, supervised by architect Brian O'Rorke, included refurbishment of the Gallery, carried out by J. F. Booth and Sons of Banbury, and Martyns of Cheltenham. The Gallery was closed for two years, to be re-opened by Sir Barry Jackson in the autumn of 1953.[198]

In the early 1980s under the guidance of the collection's curator, Brian Glover, who had previously worked for the National Museum of Wales in Cardiff, a scaffold was erected in the centre of the main gallery to make more exhibition space available and to allow an upper viewing platform to give access to pictures hung high on the walls. False walls were placed in front of the original plaster to try to eliminate the possible transfer of any damp to the pictures on display and in 1986, as the building became caught up in the evolution of the Swan Theatre, the Gallery changed its name to RSC Collection. A further re-organisation and rehang was completed in the winter of 1991-92. At this time the entrance foyer and stairway were restored to a simple decor that emphasised the elegance of the Victorian architecture.

Gallery Windows

Stained glass had been a feature of the Picture Gallery ever since its opening. To commemorate the twentieth anniversary of the foundation of the Shakespeare Memorial Theatre and also Queen Victoria's Diamond Jubilee year Edgar Flower had presented a window, which may still be seen at the head of the Gallery stairs, showing the Queen in her coronation robes. This was unveiled on 23 April 1897.

Over the years further commemorative windows have been added, related mainly to the Benson Company's time at the Stratford-upon-Avon Festival. The idea of Old Bensonian windows began in 1904 when a scheme was discussed for stained glass in the windows of what was known at the Rialto bridge between the gallery and the theatre. Actors J. T. Merridew, George Hippesley and Frank Rodney were to be commemorated but it was decided that the oriel window would be a better position. Five lights were replaced. In the centre Shakespeare's coat of arms was seen with the motto: 'We few, we happy few, we band of brothers,'[199] with two figures either side: Buckingham for Frank Rodney, then Henry V, Hotspur and Justice Shallow, each for an actor formerly in Benson's Company. The next two windows depicting Andrew Aguecheek and the Host of the Garter were added in 1905, with the glass executed by Messrs. William Pearce Limited of Bridge Street, Birmingham. The Benson Memorial Window was eventually unveiled by Sarah Flower, widow of the founder, who was introduced by a speech from actor-manager Oscar Asche on 2 May 1905. Both Frank and Constance Benson were present and the new Chairman, Archibald Flower, gave a speech of thanks.[200]

In June 1925 Dame Ellen Terry came to unveil a window on the landing, above the Juliet balcony in memory of ten Bensonians who had died in the Great War. This window was designed by F. E. Osborne and made by the craftsmen, former service-men, of Stratford-upon-Avon Guild[201] who had given the central figure of St. George the features of Frank and Constance Benson's son, Eric, killed in France in 1916. At the same time seven more panels in the oriel window, also designed by F. E. Osborne, were unveiled by actor Henry Ainley. In 1932 twelve other Old Bensonians were commemorated when Sir Frank Benson returned to inaugurate a window next to the oriel. This time the designer was Vernon Spreadbury and the work was completed by S. Wilkinson, of the Glasscraft Guild in London. Spreadbury later designed a memorial window to Sir Frank Benson himself. This showed him in the role of Richard II and it replaced the original *Henry V* quotation and the coat of arms in the centre of the oriel window. Lady Benson and Henry Ainley were commemorated at the same time and the completion ceremony was carried out by Old Bensonians, Dorothy Green and Baliol Holloway, on 24 April 1950.[202]

Phoenix-like a Swan arises

The Conference Hall was used regularly by local organisations for dances, meetings and other functions. In the winter of 1938-39 the loggia was enclosed with glass, at a cost of £1,250, to create a refreshment bar for interval use by the hall's audiences. In the same year a site for a property store was purchased from the L.M.S. railway in Old Town, Stratford, at a cost of £2,160.[203] The Conference Hall was much in demand for various charity functions in the early part of the war until the building was taken over the use as an R.A.F. canteen in 1941. There were rumours (which were only confirmed when government papers could be released fifty years later) that early in 1939 plans had been drawn up to make provision for the possibility of the government having to evacuate London if there was war with Germany. These plans made firm proposals for the relocation

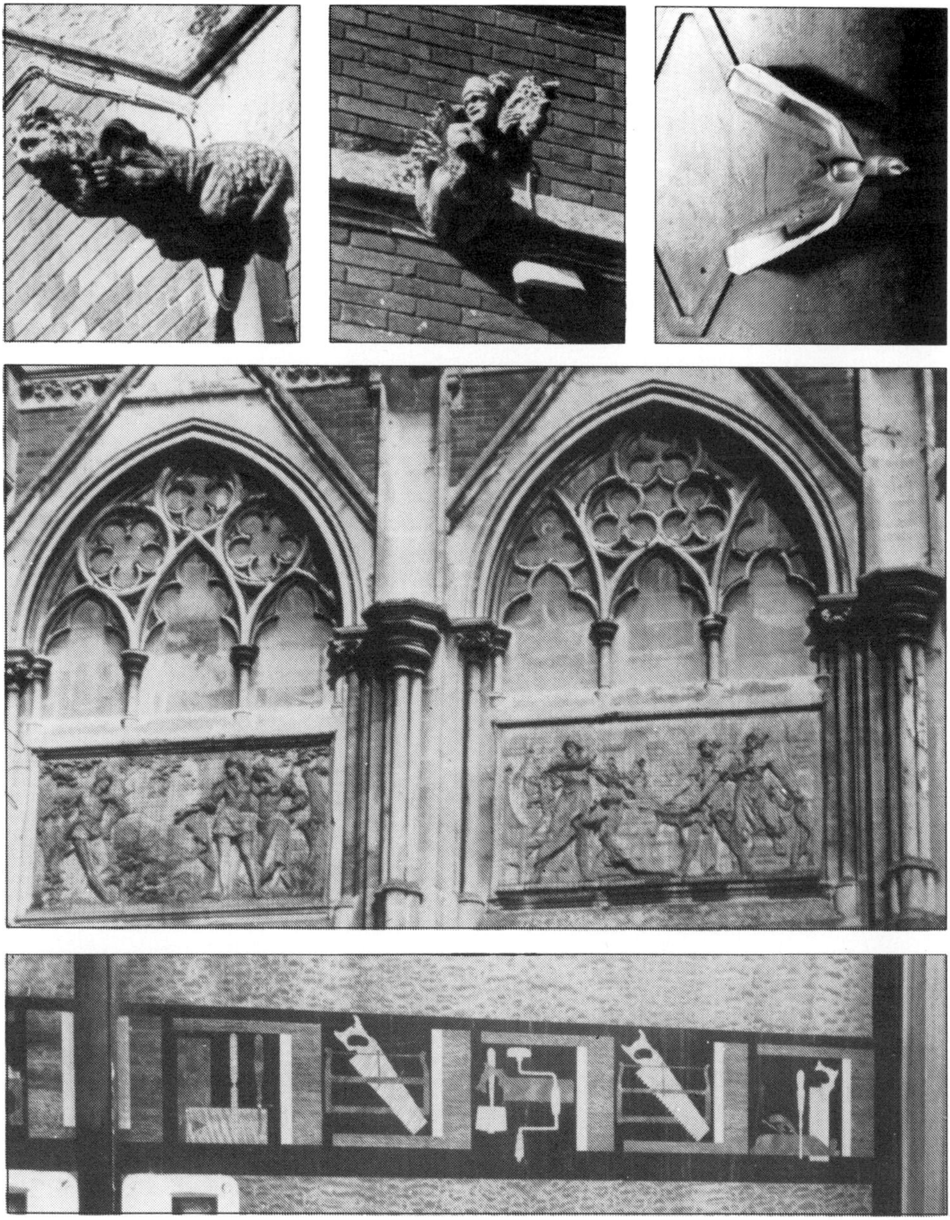

13. Some details surviving in 1993:
a) and *b)* Gargoyles (1880);
c) Hermes door handle (1932);
d) Stonework and Kummer terra-cotta panels (1880s);
e) Woodwork on restaurant entrance door, (1932).

14. a) Memorial Theatre from the river, c. 1900.

b) Swan Theatre from the gardens, 1993.

15. a) Conference Hall, c.1950.

b) Swan Theatre interior 1986 (during rehearsals for *The Fair Maid of the West.*)

16. a) The Studio, interior, 1965.

b) The Other Place, exterior, 1992.

of the House of Commons in the Shakespeare Memorial Theatre, while the House of Lords would move into the Conference Hall, with parliamentary offices in the Picture Gallery and Library building. In the event the government decided that it would not leave London unless forced to do so, and instead the theatre became a popular place of entertainment for the forces billeted in the town.[204]

After the war the Conference Hall was refurbished and Saturday dance-nights became popular; but it was decided in 1948 that the room was required by the Shakespeare festival as a permanent rehearsal room and it was seldom used for public events after this.[205] For its use as a rehearsal space the hall's acoustics were improved at a cost of £700.

In 1949, when plans for the theatre's recognition of the 1951 Festival of Britain were under discussion, Anthony Quayle prepared a special report for the theatre Governors. In this he proposed that there should be a second theatre built in Stratford which would be modelled on the public theatres of Shakespeare's London. If necessary, Quayle felt this could be a temporary structure for the 1951 Festival to be replaced later with a permanent Elizabethan stage building. He wanted it to be on the Tercentenary site, now known as the Paddock, which had been, in 1926, the alternative site for the building of the new Memorial Theatre. The Governors suggested that the Conference Hall could be converted into an Elizabethan or Globe theatre but Quayle did not wish to lose the rehearsal room and thought the Conference Hall was not suitable for the project. Architect Edward Carrick[206], in association with Brian O'Rorke, was therefore commissioned to draw up outline plans and a costing for the Paddock site.

Quayle's report to the Governors quoted the theatre critic Herbert Farjeon who had contemplated just such a theatre when the first Memorial Theatre was burned down. For Farjeon the 'right kind of theatre for Shakespeare' had no proscenium frame but had

> *a platform or apron, thrust out boldly into the auditorium so that it abolishes what would normally be the first fourteen or fifteen rows of stalls. This would be the stage, surrounded on three sides by the audience for which Shakespeare wrote his plays.*

When plans and a model were presented the following spring it was realised the project would be far too expensive and the whole proposal was dropped 'because of the urgent need to repair and improve the existing theatre.'[207]

The Conference Hall remained as the company's main rehearsal area until 1985. Trevor Nunn said that it retained the comfortable working feel of the old theatre, which, in effect, it still was in all essentials except for its flat asphalted roof.[208] After Nunn became Artistic Director of the Royal Shakespeare Company in 1968 he showed increasing interest in the idea of differing styles of theatre playing-space. The Other Place became a studio theatre of great flexibility, but the Elizabethan stages for which the plays of Shakespeare and his contemporaries were written had a fascination for Nunn. The 1976 season's permanent set of a wooden O on the Royal Shakespeare Theatre stage showed how plays could be performed with little or no scenery, and basic properties and lighting effects. The season was successful but presented a number of fire-hazard and technical problems which made it undesirable for this style of presentation to continue in the existing theatre.

A suggestion was made (reviving the long-forgotten ideas of 1949) that the Conference Hall might be converted into a public theatre, and Trevor Nunn asked scenic designer, John Napier, to prepare some drawings. The Chairman of the Governors, Sir Kenneth Cork, and his Vice-Chairman, Dennis Flower, great-nephew of the theatre's founder, and Lady Flower, widow of Sir Fordham, approved of the idea and approaches were made to local architect, Michael Reardon, who combined extensive experience in the restoration of listed buildings with theatre experience from his recently completed Riverside Studios at Hammersmith.

Reardon's brief was for a galleried auditorium with a promontory stage in the centre of an audience of 150 to 200 who would be around and above the action, and close enough to be involved in it. The resulting architect's model of a theatre conversion inside the existing Conference Hall excited all who saw it.

Tim Furby, who had previously worked as a theatre designer at Derby Playhouse and was now a member of the Reardon practice at Hillborough, near Bidford-on-Avon, was responsible for the first drawings. These did not create a reconstruction of an Elizabethan or Jacobean theatre but envisaged a new performance space embodying some of the qualities of the early theatres of Shakespeare's London which had enduring theatrical value. The inspiration for a wooden O recreated in modern terms, on which Michael Reardon and Tim Furby worked, came from the Church of Our Lord in the Attic, in Amsterdam, where the galleries appear to overhang the space below, and from the bare, unpainted woodwork at the Teatro Farnese at Parma.[209]

Some thought was given to the wooden galleries of the ducal chapel at Sabbioneta, near Mantua, in the search for a galleried interior with the necessary verticality and tension for a theatre of the kind Trevor Nunn was contemplating. The Christ's Hospital Arts Centre, near Horsham, which Nunn had visited with a small-scale RSC tour, was also considered by the architects. This is a much larger auditorium, though not so high as the Conference Hall, but it has galleried seating around a more conventional arena.[210] With these ideas in mind the proportions of the shell of the old Memorial Theatre dictated the final form of the new theatre.

The architects put their first model on view in 1978 and immediately the RSC sponsorship department set about raising the necessary £500,000. Sir Harold Wilson, then President of the RSC, went on a short fund-raising trip to New York, with Trevor Nunn. Hopes were high that the money would be found, and outline permission was granted by the local planning authority in December 1978.[211] A potential sponsor was found for the new theatre in the oil company AMOCO. They were prepared to enter into a covenant to provide the necessary funds and plans were announced to open the new theatre the following autumn with Dame Peggy Ashcroft in *All's Well That Ends Well.*

Before the financial agreement could be concluded the oil company's tanker *Amoco Cadiz* ran aground on the Brittany coast and the corporation diverted its funds to the more immediate need of responding to this ecological disaster. The funds for the new theatre could not be found elsewhere so, reluctantly, the detailed wooden scale-model was put aside in the theatre's Picture Gallery where it became a memento of yet another unfulfilled dream. The fairy-tale outcome has passed into RSC history: in 1983, an American visitor who had helped the Picture Gallery with funds in the past, saw the model in the Gallery's current exhibition. He was intrigued by the idea it embodied and, within a few days of talking to Trevor Nunn, he had agreed to provide the money needed to create the new theatre.

To begin with, the benefactor, Frederick Koch, insisted on remaining anonymous but on 13 November 1986 he shared the stage with H. M. The Queen when she formally opened the completed Swan Theatre. Koch, a Kansas oil millionaire, who was also a picture collector and supporter of the arts, had initially offered to supply the money for a building based on the Reardon/Furby model of 1978, which represented a flat-roofed theatre enclosed within the surviving parapet walls of the old Memorial building. The plans were revived in 1983 and developed by Michael Reardon Associates, but when planning permission was sought there were some objections to the proposed look of the building's exterior. The Stratford-upon-Avon Society and the Royal Fine Arts Commission disliked the imbalance between the proposed roof level and the fly tower of the Scott building. The architect quickly suggested an alternative roofline similar to that of the old Shakespeare Memorial Theatre. Far from objecting to the consequent increase in projected costs, Koch was excited by the plans and agreed to finance the whole scheme.[212] He then kept an active but unobtrusive interest in the work as it progressed. The only suggestion Koch made to change the designs was that the architects should hang the theatre lights below the gallery, or balcony, ceilings, instead of installing them in front of the galleries. This proved very much to the advantage of the final look of the theatre interior.

The shape of the new roof would now resemble that of W. F. Unsworth's Memorial Theatre when viewed from the south, but there would be a north-south ridge to connect with the mezzanine level of the fly-tower of the Royal Shakespeare Theatre.[213] In the roof space this created, Michael Reardon proposed to construct a rehearsal room which would compensate for the loss of the Conference Hall. The splendidly-proportioned new room, with magnificent views from its dormer windows over the river and the surrounding countryside, was named the Ashcroft Room in 1991 in memory of the theatre's much loved Associate Artist and member of the advisory directorate, Dame Peggy Ashcroft. Leading from the rehearsal room was a small rest room for actors, with a balcony overlooking the river. As it was not intended that the new theatre would cause any increase in the number of actors in the company, there was no need for more dressing rooms; but the space in the roof-ridge allowed for much needed offices for the maintenance wardrobe, voice director and other departments. *(Pl.14b)*

As an architect often concerned with cathedral restoration, Michael Reardon had no qualms about the building reflecting styles of different generations. He proposed a tower for the new theatre to house stairways, offices and service equipment for the air conditioning plant. This tower was placed where the old Memorial Theatre's tower had stood, but its construction, using specially handmade bricks, was in keeping with the art deco of the 1930s theatre. The old carriage-way area below the Picture Gallery bridge was to be filled in to create a foyer and public washrooms for the new theatre and, on the north side, there would be an improved stage door reception area to serve both theatres. The famous view of Shakespeare's church from the archway would be preserved by making the entrance doors of metal framed glass fitting within the archway.[214]

The new auditorium would have 'galleries' rather than balconies for seating areas. To save confusion the Picture Gallery, which would become an important factor in the new theatre project, would now be renamed the RSC Collection. The steep steps that had served the old theatre would become the main approach from the street, and the former library book stack was re-designed by Michael Reardon as an interval refreshment room that would emphasise the surviving features of the Victorian architecture. This plan, however, did not allow adequate space for the RSC Collection's reception desk and sales counter. The architect's ideas for the room were not accepted and the area remained as part of the RSC Collection, adding small counters for the sale of theatre interval drinks in the former assistant librarian and secretary's office spaces either side of the fireplace.

The original scheme for the new auditorium had envisaged a single horseshoe gallery of seats above a thrust stage with seats on three sides at floor level. However, in order to accommodate as many people as possible within a short distance of the stage, in a tense rather than a relaxed atmosphere, a second audience gallery was created, surmounted by a third gallery to house the stage management control desks and bridges for technical services. This required the walls of the shell of the old theatre to be made higher by a few courses of brick, specially handmade in the Forest of Dean to match the existing materials of the Victorian and 1930s buildings. On the river side the walls of the offices at mezzanine level were modelled on Brian O'Rorke's 1951 dressing room block below, while a corner tower for a fire escape stairway balanced Elisabeth Scott's stair tower at the north end of the complex.

Once planning permission was granted in 1985 construction began with the work being carried out by William Weaver Limited, of Bromsgrove, who had previously built the new Rose theatre at Kidderminster. The project went ahead under the guidance of project architect, Reg Ellis, and services consultant, Peter Jay. RSC Projects Administrator, James Sargant, had overall responsibility on behalf of the Company, while John Watts became Project Co-ordinator. Assistance was also given by RSC Technical Administrator, John Bradley, who designed the lighting and gave technical advice, while John A. Leonard designed sound and communications systems that gave the option of using the new theatre as a conference hall. Flexibility of performance space was allowed for by making the ground floor raked seating demountable, although it was realised that any floor level work would upset the sight-lines from the galleries above.

The new theatre's name, the Swan, was chosen for a variety of reasons. Shakespeare had been called 'Sweet Swan of Avon' by his colleague and rival dramatist, Ben Jonson. The new theatre would specialize in non-Shakespearian Elizabethan drama echoing the role of the Swan Theatre on Bankside which had been as famous in Elizabethan London as the Globe where Shakespeare's plays were staged. Since 1961, when stage designer, Lila De Nobili, had suggested a swan emblem for the new Royal Shakespeare Company, this had been a recognised symbol for the RSC and its work. This swan design was 'chosen because it was purposeful rather than romantic,' Miss De Nobili had said.[215]

The framework soon took shape within the old theatre's surrounding walls whose robust construction revealed many redundant service pipes and ducts, and whose thickness made extra insulation unnecessary. The Bradford football stadium fire disaster in May 1985 led to a tightening of fire precaution regulations in all public buildings in Britain and doubts were expressed about the wisdom of building the Swan's auditorium in timber. The architects were firm in holding out against suggestions of a steel interior construction for their galleried auditorium in favour of Douglas fir. Tests carried out on the gallery rails, once a section had been coated in a German fire retardant transparent coating, proved the timbers were far more durable than regulations demanded, so the use of fir throughout the auditorium went ahead. The fire retardant coating added about £90,000 to the cost of the building.

The new theatre was topped out on 20 December 1985 by Trevor Nunn, watched by Lady Flower and members of the acting company, and the completed Swan Theatre was ready for its audiences only two days behind schedule at the opening of the 1986 theatre season. The auditorium held 445, of which 261 were on the ground floor upholstered bench seats, with 103 (including eight standing places) in the first gallery, and 94 (including

24 standing positions) in the top gallery. The galleries not only allowed the walls of the theatre 'to be papered with people', but also actors could work from them as productions required.

The basic stage was 33 feet from the back wall to the front of the thrust and 19 feet wide. The stage floor was two feet above the auditorium floor. The rear unpainted brick wall of the stage backed onto the scene dock of the Royal Shakespeare Theatre and above the stage the height was 26 feet to the lighting bridge level. There was the option of installing galleries at either, or both, audience gallery levels to create a stage balcony for musicians or actors but there had been deliberately no request in the architects' brief for a flying option. Sets and scenery were intended to be kept to a minimum as had been the case in most playhouses of Elizabethan and Jacobean London. *(Pl.15b)*

The first play to be performed in the theatre was *The Two Noble Kinsmen,* by William Shakespeare and John Fletcher. The production brought out the flexibility and warmth of the theatre as a playing space. Winches could be used to suspend large props from the technical bridges, and the stage trap-door allowed access to and from the basement below. The first Shakespeare Memorial Theatre's extensive basement storage area had survived below the Conference Hall and had now been made damp free and watertight. The auditorium of 'bright, light, burnished wood' led Anne Fitzgerald in *Stage and Television Today*[216] to write 'Old brick and new timber make a wonderfully atmospheric combination.' 'It is an emotionally charged, intense space,' said the architect.[217]

> *The galleries are the dominating feature of the auditorium and the light-coloured wood and austere detailing of these were initially criticised by some people on the grounds that they were visually too obtrusive during the performance. The constant visual presence of this 'carpenter's work' is however, an essential component of the design.*[218]

In the main, audiences were thrilled with the theatre and the success of the first season's productions, which, by using the versatile effects of lighting, the many possibilities of entrances and exits, and a variety of approaches to design, showed how the architects had created an ideal space for the drama of Shakespeare's contemporaries. As Giles Gordon wrote in *Forte:*

By some strange process the Swan was mellow, it already had a past, a history. Notwithstanding the new, expensive, concrete homes in London of both the National Theatre and the RSC [at the Barbican] *the Swan is the most exciting theatre to have been created in Britain for a very long time. Not merely because it is handsome and attractive which it is, but because it works triumphantly.*[219]

From the outside, the south view of the theatre was a 'kind of festive tent'.[220] The roof with its ridges of rolled lead and stainless steel over the rehearsal room's timbers had been completed by a team of experts who had recently worked on York Minster's new roof on the fire damaged south transept. For various technical reasons the use of a slate roof similar to the first theatre was not feasible for the Swan and the resulting 'jousting pavilion' was finished with a roof ridge trefoil design based on a feature at the Victorian Gothic Ettington Hall, a few miles from Stratford, on which the architects had also worked. The two banner-like steel weather-vanes were designed by Anthony Robinson. He felt the RSC's swan motif was too like a chubby duck to be suitable in this position and he chose instead an image drawn from the ripples in a swan's wake on the River Avon. Robinson was also responsible for the rearing swan-shaped steel door-handles on the glass entrance to the new foyer.[221]

From the gardens you can appreciate how smoothly Michael Reardon has sculpted the new theatre from the shell of the old and - an even more difficult task - blended it into the massive brick square and rectangles of Elisabeth Scott's 1930s building wrote Anne Fitzgerald.[222]

The ivy that had been allowed to cover the Victorian theatre had been removed from the outer walls of the Conference Hall in 1946, but the wisteria, planted in Charles Edward Flower's time, had remained. It was carefully preserved during the building of the Swan, and alongside the theatre a new path down to the road was created to emerge beside the small porter's gate that survived from 1886.[223]

The Swan was unfortunately not seen by the architectural press as a new building but simply a conversion, and it featured in few professional articles. It was nevertheless recognised by the Civic Trust with an award in 1987 and eventually by the R.I.B.A. who gave it first a regional architectural award in 1988, and then a national architecture award in 1989. The theatre was given a conservation award by the Stratford-upon-Avon Society in 1987, and the internal timber fittings received a Design Prize and Civic Public Buildings award in 1987 from the National Association of Shopfitters. In January 1992 the theatre was recognised on the international architectural front when it received the prestigious Europa Nostra Award for 1991.

Since its opening season the Swan has needed little alteration. After September 1986 rails were installed on the first and second galleries to finish the standing positions, and in 1991 more seats were installed at the back of the ground floor by taking out three sections of the stalls gallery rail. The light red auditorium carpet was replaced in the winter of 1991/2 with one of a warm ochre red wool.

Initially there were some directorial worries about the intrusiveness of the auditorium, the possibility of the audience distracting attention from the stage, the difficulties of sight-lines and the problems of finding the correct focus for lighting. However, actors, directors and designers soon came to terms with the restrictions and relished its potential. As John Barton said in 1986: 'we must learn the new rules and embrace them.' In this way the company has come to exploit the building to create some of the most successful of the RSC productions of recent times. These have justified the faith of Trevor Nunn and Terry Hands in the idea of performing the plays of Shakespeare and his contemporaries and also a range of modern works in this kind of intimate space with minimal scenery.

The Other Place

When Peter Hall became director of Stratford's theatre in 1960 he established the Aldwych Theatre as the company's London base. He also proposed to lease the Arts Theatre as a studio for experimental work with actors, directors and playwrights.[224] The following March the Royal Shakespeare Company was founded and Michel Saint-Denis and Peter Brook joined Peter Hall as associate directors. Saint-Denis took responsibility for actor training and, in 1962, began work in a marquee on the lawns of Avonside (a large house owned by the theatre to the south of Holy Trinity Church), and in the Conference Hall, with movement, dance and voice sessions. Plays were also to be presented with audiences restricted to members of the theatre staff.[225]

For the next season a large corrugated-aluminium shed was put up temporarily in the Paddock in Southern Lane to replace the marquee. The plan was to move the production workshops from their old railway station site in Old Town to the Paddock and to construct a new studio theatre alongside. The Paddock had already been the home, since 1954, of the theatre's hire wardrobe department in a small wooden hut built by the theatre's own workshop staff at a cost of £2,800.[226] The new studio scheme would be paid for by selling some of the land on the site for a residential development.[227] *(Pl.16a)*

The Studio Theatre, as the project was known, would also be the venue for all understudy rehearsals. In a report to the Governors in September 1963 Saint-Denis 'regarded the studio as an absolute necessity in that it provided working conditions attractive for the assembly of a permanent company.'[228] It was intended that the following year an approach would be made to the Gulbenkian Foundation for a grant towards building a permanent theatre on the site, but Saint-Denis' ill-health led to the cancellation of these plans in November 1964.

In *Actor and Architect* in 1964, Sean Kenny wrote:

> *The theatre technicians, the actors must say 'this is what we want to begin with: a flexible space, or theatre in the round, or a stage at the side.' A new building will follow. But the architect must not come first.*

This showed that gradually more importance was being attached to the functional aspect of theatre architecture in its own right, rather than asking architects with no practical theatre experience to present or adapt familiar building styles, which, despite all the efforts of William Bridges-Adams and others, was what had happened in Stratford in the 1920s. Planners must take proper account of the experience of theatre practitioners. Kenny's sketch for a small auditorium was very similar to the kind of theatre that was eventually to emerge as the studio at Stratford-upon-Avon.[229]

The development of the Studio for the Royal Shakespeare Company in Stratford was put in the shade for a while by schemes for a new London theatre, in the Barbican Arts Centre complex, which were first discussed by the theatre Governors in September 1964 and on which the stage designer John Bury began work in May 1965.[230] In 1966 Terry Hands joined the Royal Shakespeare Company from the Liverpool Everyman Theatre to set up and run Theatregoround as an experimental educational touring group based in the tin-roofed rehearsal shed in Southern Lane beside the hire wardrobe.[231] Theatregoround had to be abandoned in 1971 but the need for a studio where small-scale work could be presented was still strongly felt by the company.

This was a decade when small theatres blossomed in Britain, and the Royal Shakespeare Company wanted

> *a theatre small enough to risk new work, in which actors could re-examine their work methods and create a different relationship with their audiences, in which seat prices could be kept down and spending on staging reduced.*[232]

In 1971 a twenty-four year-old director, Buzz Goodbody, directed *Occupations*, by Trevor Griffiths, for a brief RSC tour followed by a short season at The Place, off Euston Road in London, and two years later, with her help, a few public performances of this play were re-staged in the old Studio at Stratford.[233]

Encouraged by the success of the Studio performances, Goodbody drew up a report during the winter of 1973, in which she outlined the potential audiences and the kind of work a studio theatre could and should do in Stratford as an alternative auditorium to the Royal Shakespeare Theatre. Her enthusiasm and commitment led Trevor Nunn to appoint her as the artistic director of the new studio theatre to be named The Other Place and housed in the rehearsal studio shed.[234]

The facilities in The Other Place were minimal and for the first two years every production had different improvised seating arrangements before John Napier designed a permanent balcony around an almost square playing area with a flat floor. There was no flying space and no trap. Two extremely basic dressing rooms, one above the other, led off the only office, and there were no showers. Often actors had to brave the elements in all weathers to make entrances from the far end of the hall. Despite its drawbacks and the untimely death of Buzz Goodbody in 1975, The Other Place saw some of the company's most imaginative work on Shakespeare and a wide range of other classic and modern writers.

The Other Place attracted something of a cult-following after the production of *The Dillen* in the summers of 1983 and 1985. This play included a number of local people in the cast and consisted of peripatetic performances moving from The Other Place and its grounds to Avonbank gardens and various parts of Old Town. After this, a group of supporters formed the Friends of The Other Place to raise money for small amenities at the studio theatre. Nevertheless audiences at The Other Place had to put up with no interval facilities except an occasional icecream van or hot-dog cart in the Paddock outside, and the very limited washroom space was shared by actors and audience alike. Each year through the 1980s there were threats from the local council that the performance licence might not be renewed.[235]

A modular building was erected on the Paddock in 1985, to house rehearsals during the conversion of the Conference Hall into the Swan Theatre, and the following year the Ashcroft Room above the Swan became the principle place for rehearsal. Then the impending end of temporary planning consent for the modular rehearsal rooms created pressure to find more permanent rehearsal space leading in turn to the decision to apply for permission to redevelop the whole Paddock site. The Flower inheritance meant that the Royal Shakespeare Theatre still owned most of the buildings and land that fronted Southern Lane and now, to help raise funds, part of the ground leased to the local tennis club was sold off to the adjacent King Edward VI Grammar School. The developer, Henley and Capital Estates, purchased the ground lease of the former car-park area at the south end of the site, and plans went ahead to build thirty luxury apartments around a central courtyard in a complex that was named Avonbank Paddocks in recognition of the former ownership of the land. With the money from these projects a new Other Place could be built.

Trevor Nunn staged *Othello* as the final production in the old Other Place in the late summer of 1989, and he opened the new theatre with a production of *The Blue Angel* on 7 August 1991. After *Othello* the much-loved studio building was dismantled and sold off to become a farm building in Ireland. The hire wardrobe was moved into temporary accommodation in Old Town, near the properties workshops, and theatre architects, Michael Reardon and Tim Furby, went ahead with designing a new studio performance space which would also incorporate a rehearsal room provision. Their project architect was Greg Hamilton.

When a new Other Place was first considered in the early 1980s the architects had worked on ideas for a hexagonal or octagonal building, but decided this would look too much like a conventional arts centre. Various drawings were made and talks were held with the Royal Shakespeare Company's General Manager, David Brierley, and with Trevor Nunn and Terry Hands, the two Artistic Directors. At the time there seemed little prospect of finding the money required and, when the Swan Theatre project intervened the studio plans were shelved.

When the plans were revived in 1988 the Friends of the Other Place argued strongly for not altering the basic plan of their beloved studio. Finally it was decided by the planning group who included the Administrator of The Other Place, Bronwyn Robertson and RSC Projects Administrator, James Sargant, that the best possible configuration for the new theatre was the simple style of the old tin hut, where the audience entered straight from the street into the auditorium. The site finally chosen, with its entrance directly off Southern Lane, almost opposite the ferry, was the third position to be considered. This was selected partly for its relationship to the eighteenth-century timber and brick grain barn on the site, which Reardon could convert into an interval refreshment area with an actors' rest room, or green room, upstairs. A new building here would leave ample space at the back for a car-park and for access by scene-removal vehicles.

The new performance space had a stage floor 9 metres by 13 metres, which was slightly larger than that of the first studio. The audience was seated on three sides, with the option of the fourth side being available. There were up to three rows of upholstered bench seating downstairs and two rows of similar black fabric covered seats on a three-sided gallery above. The old Other Place had seated 160 at the most, while in the new theatre there was room for 240, or up to 270 if all four sides were used.[236] The whole was intended to be very close in look and feel to John Napier's designs from the 1970s. Beyond the stage area, facing the entrance, was a scene dock, with direct access to the parking area, and below was a T-shaped pit trap with its own approach channel leading from the dock. The placing of the audience entrance to face the back of the stage, rather than on the side wall as in the old Other Place, moved the configuration through ninety degrees and gave the architects a much easier and more logical plan for the other parts of the building. *(Pl.16b)*

The new theatre would have three entrances onto the playing floor from each side, both at ground level and on the first floor. To the south of the auditorium there was to be a wide corridor on the ground floor from which led a maintenance wardrobe room and offices. Two rehearsal rooms, each named after one of the founders of The Other Place, were built at the end of this corridor. The Buzz Goodbody rehearsal room was the size of The Other Place, and was intended for studio theatre rehearsals, while the Michel Saint-Denis room allowed full-scale rehearsals for the Swan Theatre stage. In the rehearsal rooms there were no balconies or galleries, but tall windows, high ceilings and acoustic panels in pine and red cloth made them good atmospheric spaces for creative working. These rooms left the Ashcroft Room at the Swan available for rehearsals for the Royal Shakespeare Theatre's larger stage. Upstairs in the new building, leading from a second wide corridor, there were two dressing rooms each for five actors, and one for ten actors, as well as two shower rooms. Office space and a production wardrobe store completed the complex.

The building's cost was severely restricted by the funds available from the sale of the lease of the adjacent development site, and a few minor modifications had to be made to the plans. The move of services and air-conditioning plant into a small tower above the dressing rooms released roof space for technical bridges and lighting positions above the auditorium without these being visible or intrusive. The lighting and control rooms were placed above the audience entrance, and two stairways (instead of four in the old Other Place) gave access to the gallery seating level. The reduction in internal stairways was achieved by having an exterior fire-escape from the seating gallery into the car-park.

The Other Place was built in local red brick by Kevin Gildea Limited of Warwick, with Dudley Port Steel Structures Limited and Tipton Bigwood Brothers of Birmingham providing the framework and roof. The whole building was completed within a budget of £1.5 million. This was achieved with the aid of the Other Place practice of re-using old lighting units from the previous building, or cast-offs from the better provided Royal Shakespeare Theatre two hundred yards down the road.

When the first audiences assembled in August 1991 they were surprised and pleased at how similar in looks, atmosphere and intimacy the new theatre was to their memories of the old auditorium. The interior steel was painted black while, to be unobtrusive, walls throughout the building were for the most part unpainted. The balcony was suspended from above, instead of resting on the floor, and the resulting absence of support pillars that had blocked sight-lines in the old Other Place was much approved. The tremendous flexibility of the new building was fully tested when in

October 1991, an *avant garde* musical version of *King Lear*, from the Tokyo Shakespeare Globe, was staged for three performances as part of the British Japan Festival.

Michael Reardon could rightly be pleased that the new Other Place fulfilled its expectations. 'I confess', he said, 'that I get most satisfaction from buildings that are obviously used and enjoyed by people who probably give little thought to their aesthetic merits.'[237] Backstage the great advantages in the new building have been much appreciated, not least the social opportunities. The Other Place soon became a popular daytime meeting place for actors, whereas in the old building there had been no reason to be on the premises unless work was in progress. In the months following its completion the courtyard approach to the new theatre was enhanced by seats and planting presented by the Friends of the Other Places, who had by this time changed their name to show their support for the Swan Theatre as well as the studio.

As The Other Place was completed James Sargant reflected:

> *It is interesting that on both the Swan and Other Place projects, problems of finance brought us to a standstill for two years or more when the first design stage had been reached. On both occasions when we were able to begin again, Michael* [Reardon] *decided to go right back to the beginning. In both cases, mark two greatly benefited from the fresh start, gaining in both design concept and in economical use of the available site.*[238]

EPILOGUE

Gradually, over the years, Stratford's Shakespeare memorial has developed into what has been called 'a rather collegiate collection of buildings'[239] which help create a functioning unity for the Royal Shakespeare Company. Charles Edward Flower's motto had been: 'To conquer or die', and a century later Fordham Flower, on his knighthood, selected the motto: 'Et Flores et Fructus.' The founder conquered the considerable opposition to his Shakespeare memorial scheme and his great-nephew saw its flowering into a company of international renown that has brought world-wide fame and esteem to Stratford-upon-Avon.

The company's three Stratford auditoria, the Royal Shakespeare Theatre, the Swan and The Other Place all differ significantly in what they require from the professionals who work in them, and from their audiences. In so doing they complement one another and offer the same actors and directors, who work in all three spaces, the opportunity of presenting drama over the widest possible spectrum.

Elisabeth Scott's theatre was opened the year after the Empire State Building was completed and within a few months of Eric Gill finishing work on his statue of Prospero and Ariel for the BBC's new Broadcasting House in London. The 1930s was a time of architectural innovation in which new materials were used with artistic inventiveness. It was a time also for women to demonstrate their abilities. In the spirit with which Amy Johnson first flew solo from London to Australia in 1931, so Elisabeth Scott dared to use her talents to bring together sculptors, painters and interior designers to provide a memorable and fitting setting for the presentation of the works of the greatest dramatist of the English-speaking world.

The architecture of the first Memorial Theatre was officially recognised for its Victorian Gothic value when the remaining walls and the Gallery wing were given Listed Building Grade II status in 1971. Elisabeth Scott's work was granted the same grade of listing on 14 October 1980, at the same time as two near contemporary buildings, Battersea Power Station and the Hoover factory in London's Western Avenue. In 1993 the listing for the whole site has been upgraded to II*.

The creation in the last few years of the Swan and the new Other Place has been another major milestone in the long history of theatre buildings in Stratford-upon-Avon. Like their predecessors they have made a distinctive contribution to the architectural heritage of the town, at the same time as extending the possibilities for audiences to enjoy Shakespeare's plays where they belong first and foremost, on the stage. We should remember the aims of the founders of the Memorial in also using the visual and tactile arts to honour the poet's name in the buildings where he is celebrated.

Afterword

No building of this kind ever stands still. Since completion of this history in the autumn of 1992 the Royal Shakespeare Theatre has been extensively refurbished under the direction of Michael Reardon, with design assistance from Tim Furby. The auditorium was completely reseated in modern upholstered unit seats by Quinette Gallay International of Montreuil, France and the balcony benches were replaced by simple individual fold-down seats. The auditorium's demountable unit seats allow for up to six wheelchair spaces to be available according to demand, instead of the two backstall positions previously provided. The rustic bamboo chairs that had furnished the circle bar for several years were moved into the dress circle boxes to allow more flexible seating and the circle foyer was supplied with Quinette Gallay seats to match the auditorium.

All the new seating was installed by Audience Systems of Westbury, Wiltshire, in February to March 1993. The fabric colour of pale violet was continued with redecoration of the walls and ceiling in Dulux Queens velvet in shades of purple and violet with 'black pearl' fabric baffles. At the same time the balcony slips were re-fronted with rails to Furby's designs made by Genesis Ltd. to match the dress circle installations of 1988. New 'art deco'-style wall-fittings, designed by Spanish architect Ricardo Bofil, were made in Belgium for Futumis of Harlow in Essex who carried out their installation. A permanent prompt corner for the Deputy Stage Manager was created at the end of the west side (audience right) of the circle.

Backstage modifications were carried out to improve the main office corridor and general administration office and changes of use in office accommodation allowed the creation of four new dressing-rooms. At the front-of-house the much-worn stair-treads of the main staircase were skillfully renewed with Hornton stone, inset with a white edge-strip, for added safety. Part of the stalls bar entrance floor, and the floor of the River-Room were re-tiled with Anglo-Italia tiling in shades of dark red and green to match the decor carried out the previous year. This work was completed in March 1993 and a few weeks later an information and visitor reception desk, designed by Andrew Shenton of Todenham, was created in the foyer in front of the cloakroom. The timber for this desk matched that of the sales desks for the shop and for programmes, that had been built the previous year.

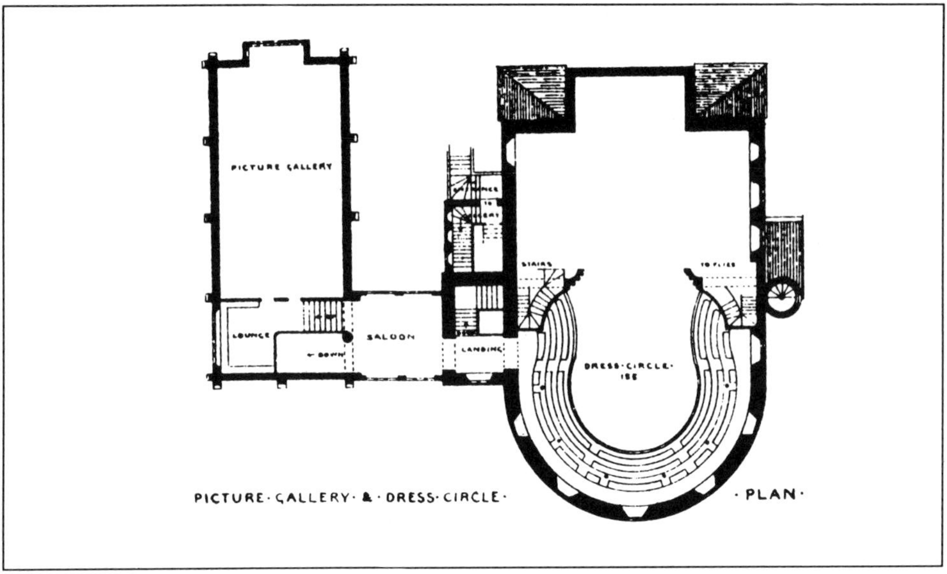

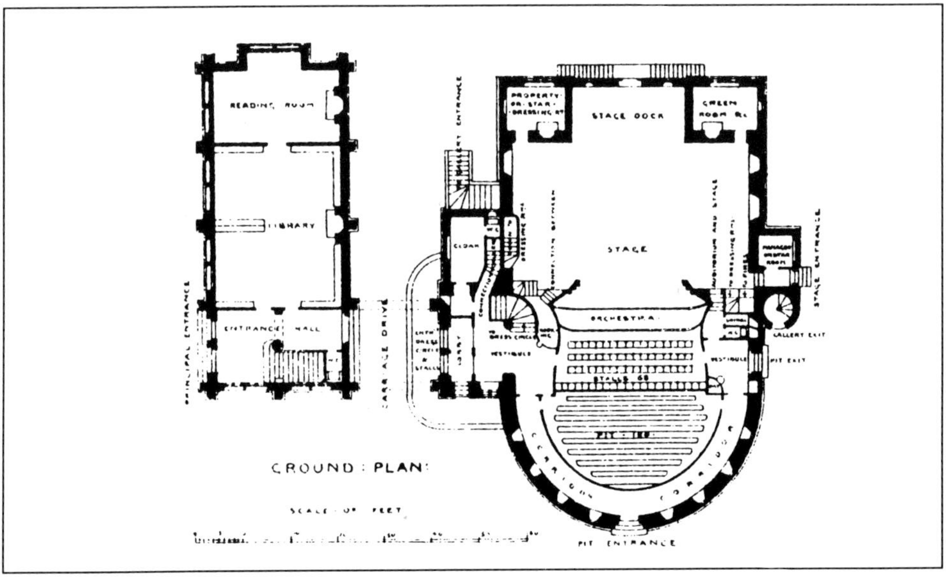

Plan 1. The Shakespeare Memorial Theatre, 1879.

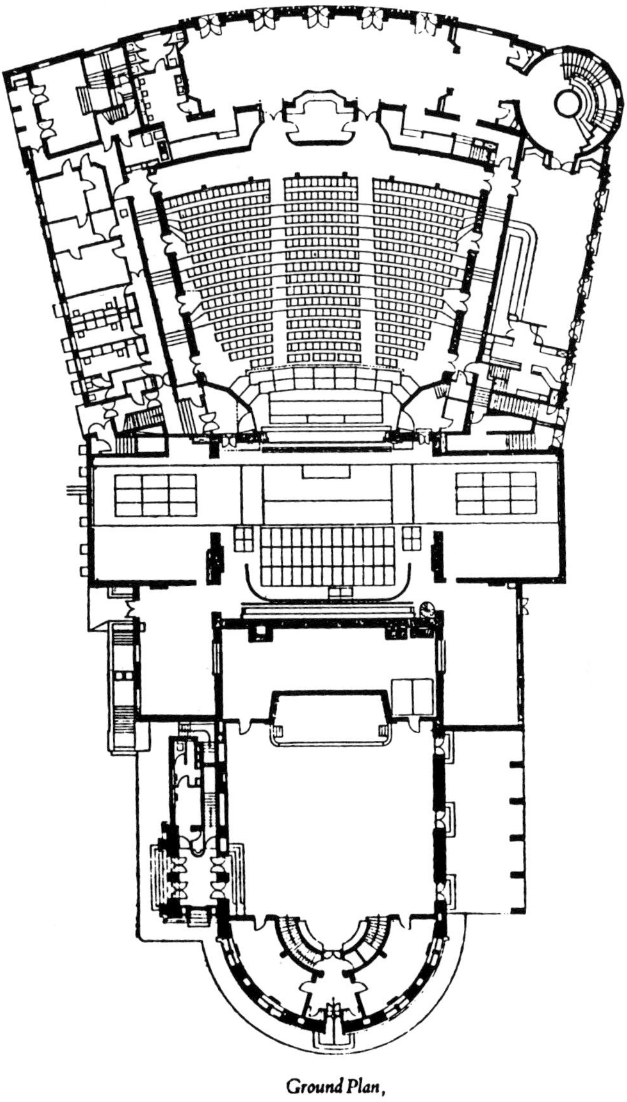

Plan 2. 1932 Ground plan, showing surviving parts of the first theatre.

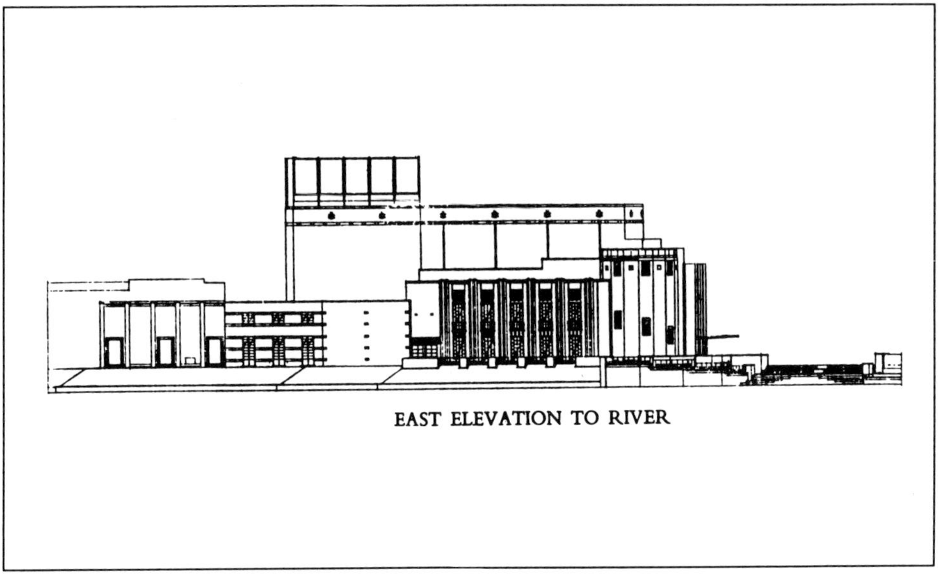

Plan 3. a) East elevation to river, 1932.

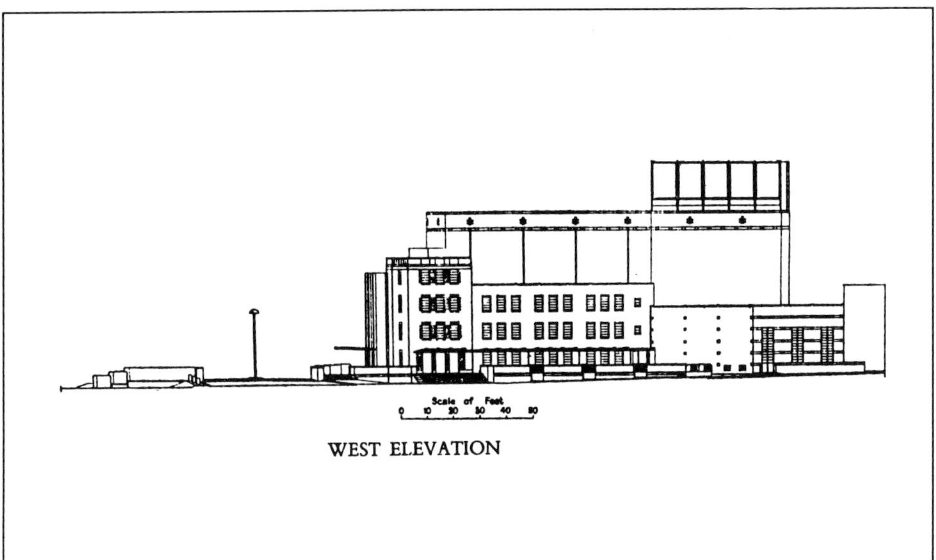

Plan 3. b) West elevation, 1932.

6. Sounding board
8. Proscenium Opening
11. Acoustic Splays with doors
12. Plaster ceiling & lighting troughs
13. Dress Circle restaurant
14. Stalls refreshments
15. Actor's dressing room
16. Star dressing room
17. Orchestra room
18. Stalls Exit passage
21. Supers' dressing rooms
25. Roof flat

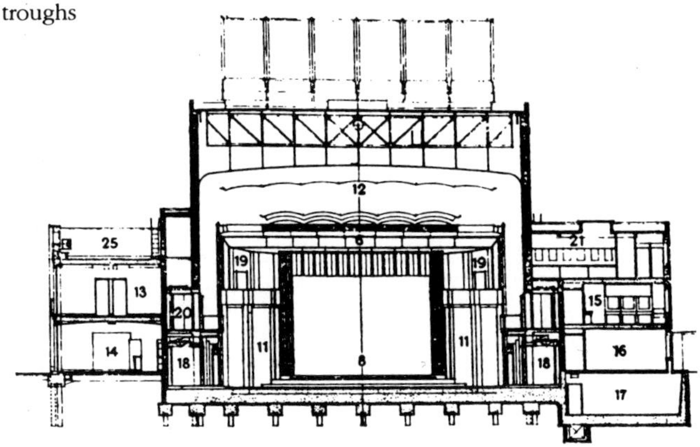

CROSS SECTION THROUGH AUDITORIUM

3. Fireproof Curtain and Proscenium Opening
4. Bridges
22. Bays for rolling stages
23. Mess room
24. Space for flying scenery
25. Roof flat

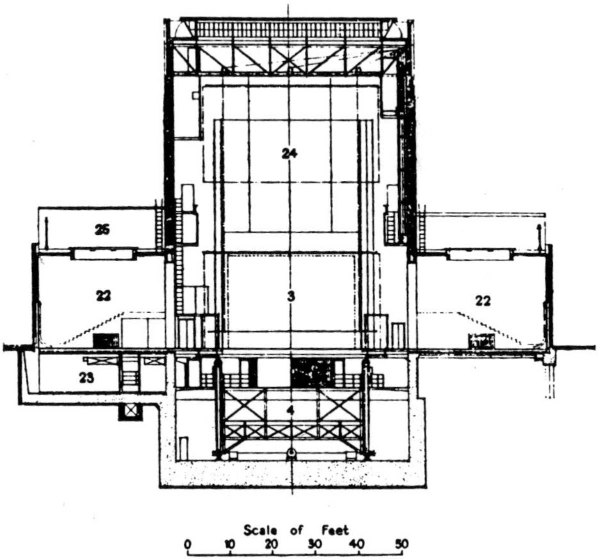

CROSS SECTION THROUGH STAGE

Plan 4.

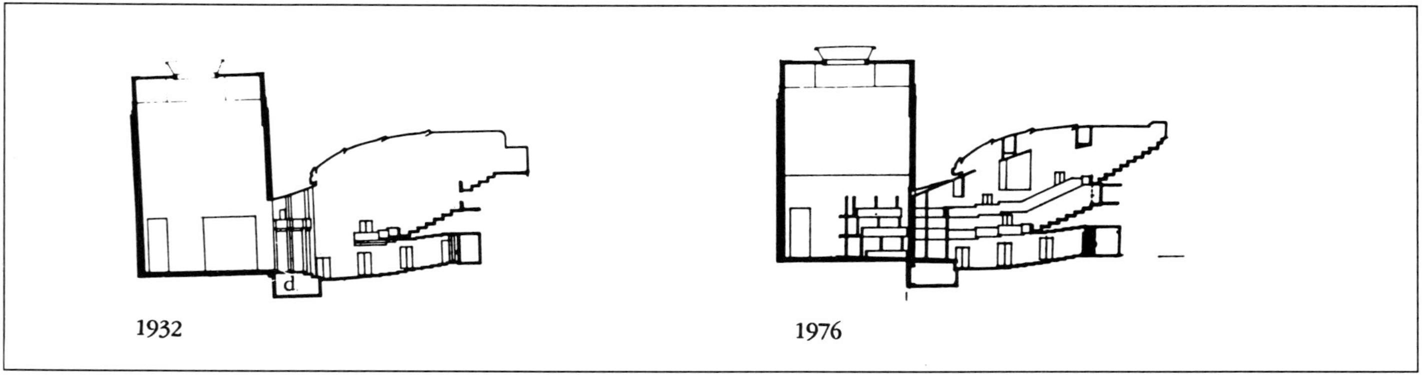

Section through fly-tower and auditorium

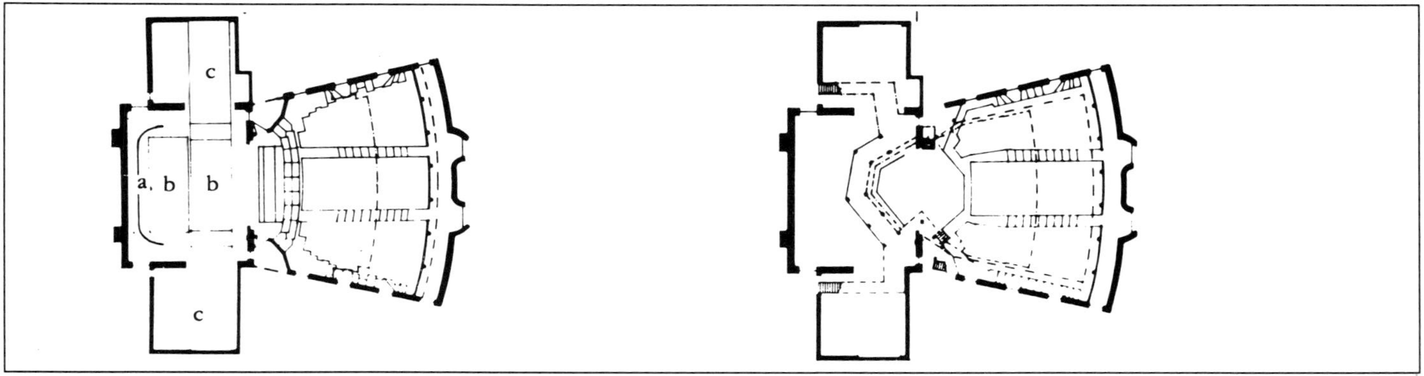

Auditorium and stage ground floor plan.

a. cyclorama, b. stage lifts, c. rolling stages, d. orchestra pit.

Note dress circle extensions (1951)
& side balcony and slips (1972)

Plan 5. Comparative sections and plans, 1932/1976. (Iain Mackintosh).

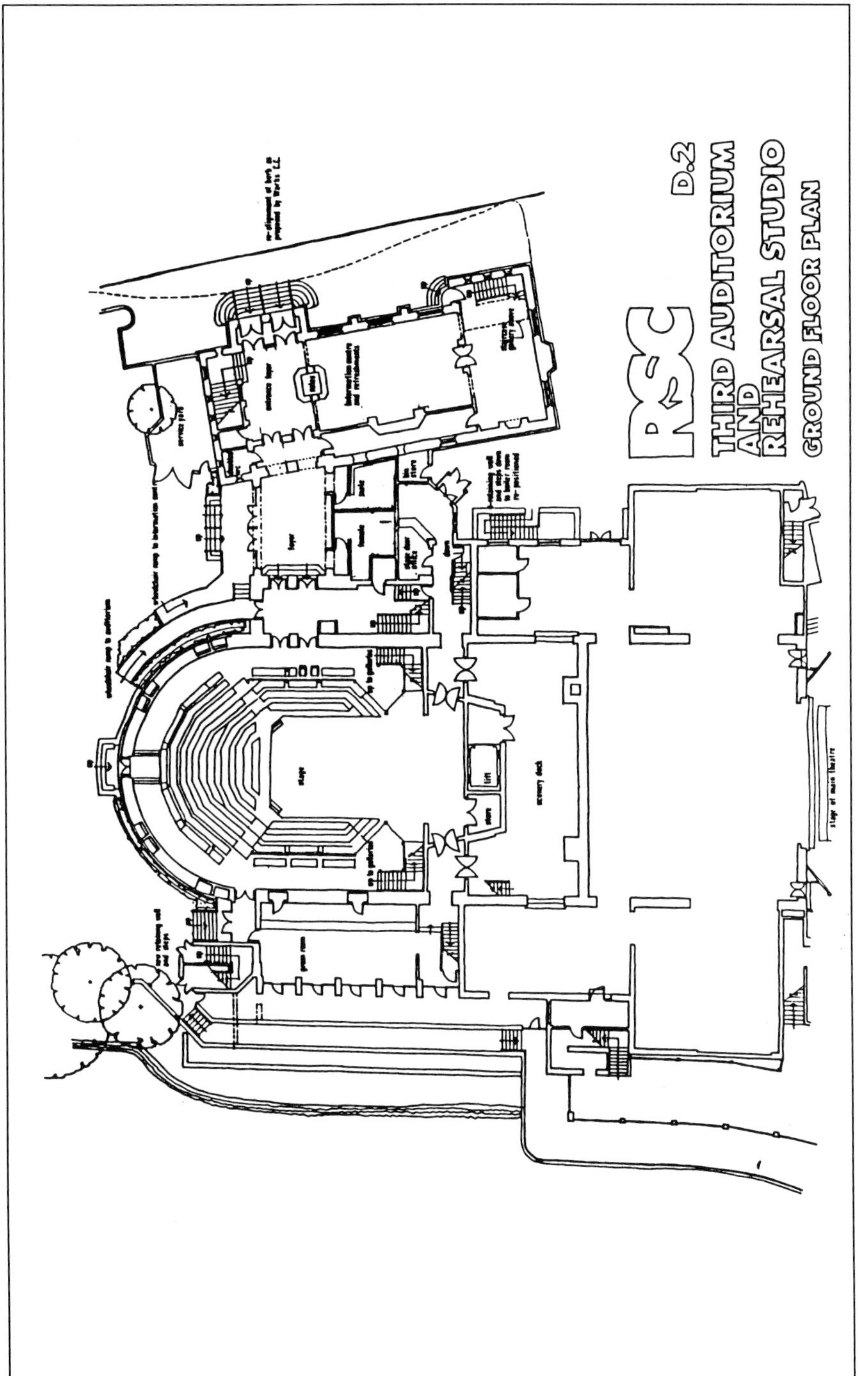

Plan 6. Swan Theatre ground plan, 1985 (Michael Reardon & Associates)

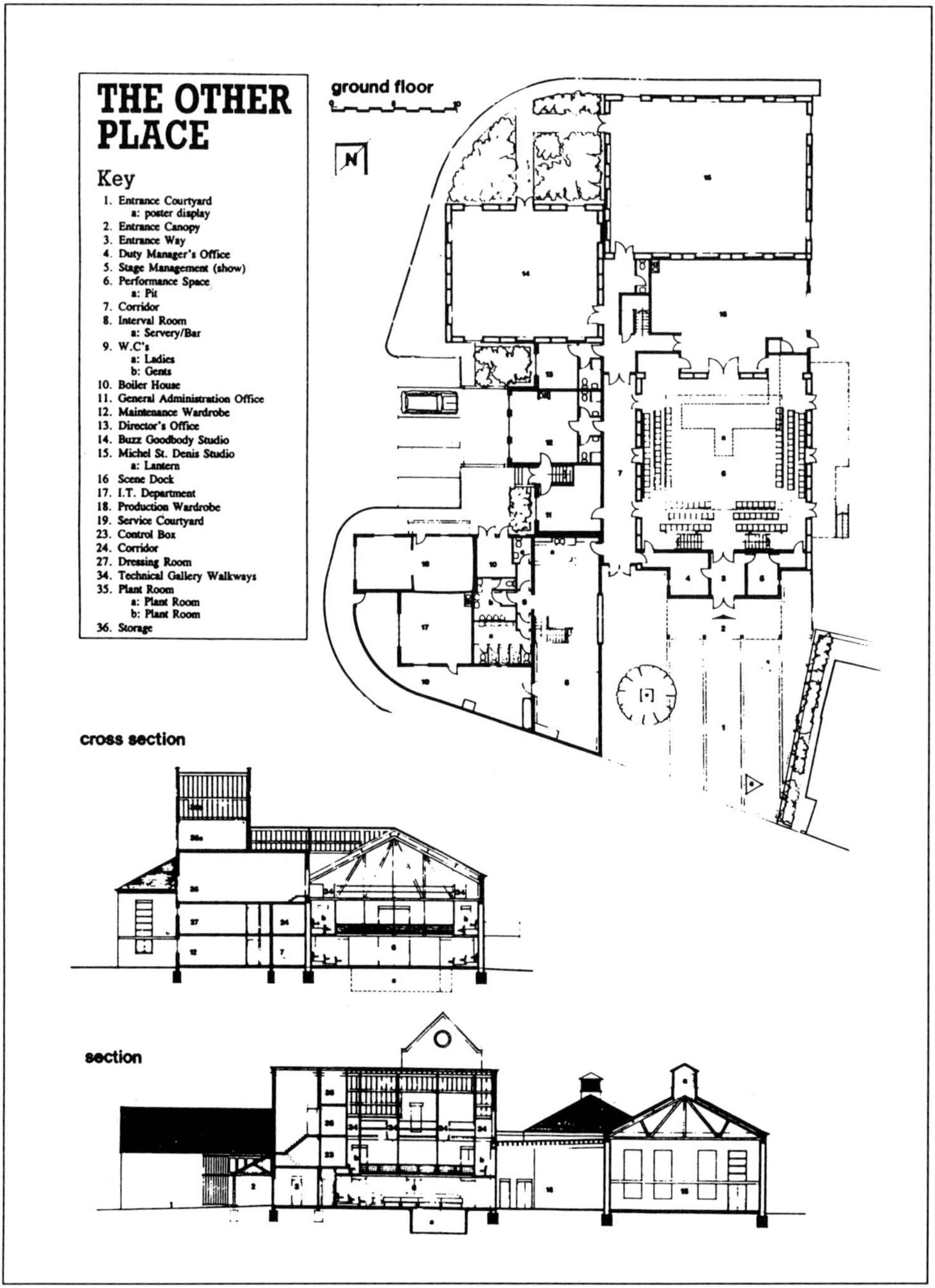

Plan 7. The Other Place, 1991. (Michael Reardon & Associates)

NOTES

Key: For S.M.T. read Shakespeare Memorial Theatre
For R.S.C. read Royal Shakespeare Company
For S.B.T. read Shakespeare Birthplace Trust
For S.C.L. read Shakespeare Centre Library

Place of publication of all books is London, unless otherwise stated.

Theatre Records is the Royal Shakespeare Theatre Library's series of scrapbooks of newscuttings relating to the S.M.T. from 1875 onwards. These are housed at the Shakespeare Centre Library, Stratford-upon-Avon.

1. T. C. Kemp and J. C. Trewin *The Stratford Festival. A History of the Shakespeare Memorial Theatre* (Birmingham, 1953); Sally Beauman *The Royal Shakespeare Company. A History of Ten Decades* (Oxford, 1982).
2. For example see record of 12 January 1586/7 in: *Minutes and Accounts of the Corporation of Stratford-upon-Avon,* transcribed by Richard Savage, v, 1586-92 (Dugdale Society x, 1929), p. 32.
3. The Unicorn at 5-6 Wood Street was an inn from 1632 to 1774. The hostelry of this name, near Clopton Bridge, which was renamed the Pen and Parchment in the early 1980s, was not known as the Unicorn before 1786.
4. Also known as the Woolpack.
5. Moor Town's End is now Greenhill Street.
6. This building, later a garage and then a bicycle shop, was finally demolished to make way for new development in the 1950s.
7. For further details of Stratford's early theatres see the *Victoria County History of Warwickshire*, iii, (1945) pp. 28-30: 'The Borough of Stratford-upon-Avon and Alveston', by Philip Styles, and playbills in S.C.L.; for the Garrick Jubilee details see Christian Deelman *The Great Shakespeare Jubilee* (1964). The story of the theatre, later also known as the Royal Shakespearean Rooms, in Chapel Lane is recorded in *Aris's Birmingham Gazette* for 4 May 1872 preserved in *Theatre Records*, i, p.2.
8. See Richard Foulkes *The Shakespeare Tercentenary of 1864* (1984). The remaining sum of £177 2s 5d from the Tercentenary account was paid to the Shakespeare Memorial Association for the new theatre before 1879.
9. In 1991 Avonbank Paddocks apartments were built around a courtyard on this historic site. For further details see later. For a biography of Charles Edward Flower see Beauman *op.cit.* pp.8-11.
10. Another design was submitted by Sir Matthew Digby Wyatt, the former Secretary of the Royal Institute of British Architects. For details of the proposed monument see *Builder,* 7 October 1865; Robert Bearman *The Market House* (Stratford-upon-Avon, 1990) pp.16-19; and R. Foulkes *op.cit.* p.49.
11. The original drawings for this plan survive in S.C.L.
12. This letter was re-published in March and April 1875, with lists of the subscribers to the scheme to date.

13. S.M.T. Minute book 1, also: Beauman *op.cit.* p.12, and an account of Council Meeting 7 October 1874, in *Stratford-upon-Avon Herald*, concerning the purchase of land by C. E. Flower for public gardens and for his own use at Avonbank.
14. S.C.L. Shakespeare Association Box 1.
15. *Stratford-upon-Avon Herald*, 3 March 1876. 'What here shall Miss ...' is from *Romeo and Juliet*, Prologue, l.14.
16. *Stratford-upon-Avon Herald*, 3 March 1876.
17. *Leamington Spa Courier*, 11 March 1876.
18. The decoration for this design was described in the *Architect*, 29 April 1876.
19. *Leamington Spa Courier*, 11 March 1876.
20. *Building News*, 3 March 1876, p.213.
21. *Stratford-on-Avon Chronicle*, 28 April 1876.
22. *Building News*, 15 September 1876. E. M. Barry's work included Covent Garden Opera House (1857-59), the Birmingham and Midland Institute (1855), the Birmingham Public Library (1861, demolished 1970) and Great Ormond Street Hospital for Sick Children (1872-76).
23. *Building News*, 7 July 1876. 'But to the purpose ...' is from *Henry IV, Part 2*, Epilogue, l.17.
24. In *Building News*, 22 September 1876.
25. John Bott *The Figure of the House* (Stratford-upon-Avon, 1974)
26. Obituary *RIBA Journal*, xxxiv, 2 April 1927, and A. Stuart Gray *Edwardian Architecture* (1985),p.165
27. Triggs (1876-1923), see Gray *op.cit.*, p.356.
28. The chapel was begun in the 1880s. See A. F. Leach *History of Warwick School* (1906) p.229.
29. Obituary *RIBA Journal*, xix, 19 October 1912; Peter Bennett *A Very Desolate Position* (priv. print., 1991)
30. J. Mills was to be paid £2 a week.
31. The highest tender was £14,800 cf. S.M.T. Minute Book 1.
32. 'Whilst it cannot be confirmed that Charles Edward Flower was a Freemason, his nephew, Sir Archibald Flower, who was to be the moving spirit of the 1929 venture, certainly was.' See Paul Morgan 'The Shakespeare Memorial Theatre and freemasonry.' In *Warwickshire Masonic Record*, ix, October 1985. For details of the collection see S.C.L. Shakespeare Association Box 1.
33. *Stratford-upon-Avon Herald*, 27 September 1878, and 17 January 1879.
34. *Leamington Courier*, 12 October 1878.
35. Edward Fox *Fox Penny Guide to Stratford-on-Avon* [Stratford-upon-Avon, 1898].
36. *Daily Telegraph*, 21 March 1877; Bott, *op.cit.*
37. *Birmingham Daily Gazette*, 9 March 1876.
38. *Funny Folks*, 17 November 1877.
39. *Daily Telegraph*, 21 March 1879; *Stratford-upon-Avon Herald*, 28 March

1897.

40. This was of little use when fire destroyed the theatre in March 1926.
41. *Stratford-on-Avon Chronicle*, 8 April, 1881.
42. The designs for the terracotta panels were illustrated in *Building News*, 4 July 1889.
43. Bott *op.cit.* p.10; and C. E. Flower *A History of the Shakespeare Memorial* (2nd ed., 1882)
44. The stonework style shows the influence of the guilds of handicraft that grew up after John Ruskin founded the Guild of St. George in the 1870s, and which blossomed in the Arts and Crafts movement of the 1880s.
45. S.M.T. Minute Book 1, 11 June 1881.
46. S.M.T. Minute Book 1, 24 April 1882.
47. *Stratford-upon-Avon Herald*, 13 April and 19 October 1883.
48. *Stratford-upon-Avon Herald*, 18 October 1883.
49. Edwin O. Sachs *Modern Opera Houses and Theatres*, iii (1897) p.42.
50. S.M.T. Minute Book 1, 17 July 1885.
51. S.M.T. Minute Book 1, 28 April 1886.
52. S.M.T. Minute Book 1, April 23 1883 and *Stratford-upon-Avon Herald*, 20 July 1883.
53. Robert Bearman *Stratford-upon-Avon. A History of its Streets and Buildings* (1988).
54. Certificate in S.C.L. Shakespeare Association Box 1.
55. S.M.T. Minute Book 1, 5 May 1887.
56. 2 July 1888 S.C.L. Shakespeare Association Box 1.
57. Michael Kimberley *Lord Ronald Gower's Monument to Shakespeare* (Stratford-upon-Avon, 1989).
58. S.M.T. Minute Book 1, 15 October 1888.
60. *Leamington Spa Courier*, 12 October 1878.
61. Sachs *op.cit.* p.42.
62. *Birmingham Post*, 11 October 1888.
63. M. C. Day and J. C. Trewin *The Shakespeare Memorial Theatre* (1932), p.41.
64. S.M.T. Minute Book 1, 28 April 1886; and see S. Beauman *op.cit.* p.17 and note p.356. The cottages on Waterside given by Charles Flower still belong to the theatre today and the RSC's Production Wardrobe department is housed in part of the premises.
65. Subscribers list published in C. E. Flower *A History of the Shakespeare Memorial* (2nd ed. 1882) pp.22-39.
66. W. Bridges-Adams who ran the festivals from 1919 to 1935 commented that the design showed 'the place which Shakespeare and the Bible holds in the English mind.' *Daily News* 20 April 1920.
67. *Stratford-upon-Avon Herald*, January 1879; there is an account of the Beverley act-drop in S.C.L. at P.C.71.2 Int 1879.
68. *Stratford-on-Avon Chronicle*, 21 March 1879.
69. Sarah Flower *Great Aunt Sarah's Diary, 1846-1892.* (priv. print. 1964) S.B.T.

Records Office.

70. *The Times* and the *Daily Telegraph*, 24 and 25 April 1879.
71. S.M.T. Minute Book 1, 18 October 1880.
72. Shakespeare Memorial Association Annual Report 1904.
73. S.M.T. Minute Book 1, 28 April 1886.
74. Arthur Smyth Flower, F.R.I.B.A., F.S.A., (1860-1936) was the son of Sir William Henry Flower, founder of the Natural History Museum in Kensington.
75. The *Builder*, 29 June 1889, published plans and a description of this building.
76. Papers in S.B.T. Records Office at DR344/13-43.
77. S.M.T. Annual report, 1907.
78. Geoffrey A. Jellicoe *The Shakespeare Memorial Theatre* (1933) p.vii.
79. *Stratford-upon-Avon Herald*, 27 January 1882.
80. *Architect and Building News*, April 1932; *Stratford-upon-Avon Herald*, 25 April 1876.
81. S.C.L. *Theatre Records* i. p.33, February 1880.
82. *Stratford-upon-Avon Herald*, 24 April 1925. Shaw criticised the uncomfortable seats and lack of ventilation, and emphasised the need for 'a properly equipped modern stage.' For the best account of the fire see Day and Trewin *op.cit.* pp.178-187. A. Flower quoted in *Midland Daily Telegraph* 8 March 1926.
83. The Picture House was demolished in 1983 to make way for Safeway's supermarket. See James Sargant 'Five weeks and two days', in *Sightline*, xvii, no 2 Autumn 1983; see also Susan Brock and Marian J. Pringle *The Shakespeare Memorial Theatre 1919 to 1945* (1984), pp.26 and 102.
84. See Beauman *op.cit.* p.245.
85. *Birmingham Mail*, 5 January 1928.
86. Fordham Flower 'A New History', in S.M.T. Season Souvenir 1959, p.8; Granville Barker was a leading supporter of the kind of theatre Archie Flower wished to establish at Stratford. He was a founder member of the Shakespeare Memorial National Theatre Association. His strongly held views on the purpose and projected working methods of a national theatre were set out in *The Exemplary Theatre* (1922) and in *A National Theatre* (1930).
87. See Archibald Flower to Harley Granville-Barker, 20 April 1926, Letter 3 of Correspondence in S.C.L. (S.R./M.S. 71.2).
88. Letter 28, 13 October 1926, and Letter 6, 21 May 1926, of correspondence cited above. The oval part of the orangery, designed by Henry Hakewell, was the only surviving part of the first Avonbank, the hunting villa of Lord Middleton, which Charles Edward Flower had demolished to build his own house on the riverside in Southern Lane. See William Smyth *History of the County of Warwick* (1830), illustration facing p.266. A Flower family album survives in S.C.L. containing many original drawings by architect F. C. Penrose, and photographs of Avonbank and the orangery which has a

pediment that came from the College, in nearby Mill Lane (demolished 1799).

89. Harley Granville-Barker to Archibald Flower, Letter 9, 8 July 1926.

90. E. Guy Dawber (1861-1938) had wide experience of designing all kinds of public buildings from chapels and village halls to golf clubs and country houses, but he had never before worked on a theatre.

91. Harley Granville-Barker to Archibald Flower, Letter 28, 13 October 1926; *Recommendations of the Advisory Committee* were published in October 1926.

92. For a summary of the competition conditions see Brock and Pringle *op.cit.* pp.108-9, also see *ibid.* p.33.

93. *Architect and Building News*, 22 April 1932.

94. *Architect and Building News*, 22 April 1932; Robert Atkinson (1883-1952) had experience of building cinemas in the early years of his practice with Alexander and Atkinson, 1914-1918; Raymond Hood (1881-1934) was architect of the American Radiator Building and the *Daily News* building in New York. Over 120 architects paid the one guinea fee for competition details which was refunded to those who did not submit drawings. Details of the architects' names survive in S.M.T. archive Box 1, S.C.L., where certified letters from the six finalists claiming sole responsibility for their competition entries also remain. Scott = no.5, Rousseau = 27, Percy Tubbs = 31, Martin-Smith = 37, Derrick = 64 and Moscowitz = 72.

95. Robert O. Derrick was later to design the Henry Ford Museum in Dearborn, Michigan, while Rousseau, who was Professor of Architecture at the University of Michigan at Ann Arbor, and the other American finalists had no major buildings to their names. The Percy Tubbs partnership designed and built several public buildings in London in the 1930s including Barclays Bank in Sloane Square, and the *Glasgow Herald* newspaper office. In 1937 S. Rowland Pierce was responsible for new Urban District Council Offices in Slough. *Burnham Index to Architectural Literature* (New York, 1989); also RIBA Library Grey Book, and Jellicoe *op.cit.* p.7; photographs of all the finalists' plans are in S.C.L. at P.C.71.2/1927.

96. Although it was never officially announced D.F. Martin-Smith's entry was the runner-up. S.C.L. P.71.2/1927 report.

97. Sir Giles Gilbert Scott (1880-1960) won the competition for Liverpool Anglican cathedral when he was 22. The contract for this building began in 1903. He also built the University Library for Cambridge, London's Waterloo Bridge which opened in 1945, and Battersea Power Station. He was knighted in 1924 and created O.M. in 1944.

98. *Architects' Journal*, xv, 12 July 1972. Maurice Chesterton (1883-1962) was a cousin of the writer G.K. Chesterton. His work before the association with Scott and Shepherd had included a remarkable circular thatched dairy farm, The Node, at Codicote in Hertfordshire, (1928). See *Country Life* 18 December 1980, p.2333, and *Builder*, ccii, p.6213, 15 June 1962. Later,

during the war Chesterton moved to Suffolk where he worked on housing schemes for Samford District Council at Tattingstone and at Stratford St. Mary. He retired in the 1950s. His daughter, Dame Elizabeth Chesterton, A.R.I.B.A. recalls:

> *My father made a point of always saying that he had nothing to do with designing the theatre. But I know that he had everything to do with researching stage requirements, fire and health and safety requirements, negotiations with the client fund raisers and the many specialists who were involved. In short, he was responsible for seeing the contract through in all its aspects.* - Letter to the author, March 1993.

John Chiene Shepherd (1896-1978) was partner to Geoffrey Jellicoe with whom he had trained at the Architectural Association. Shepherd was courting Scott's flatmate when he saw the drawings for the competition and added his suggestions, including the tower and the interior staircase at the north-east corner. It was these designs that helped to win the competition for Scott. To work on the theatre project Shepherd gave up his work with Jellicoe who went on to become a successful landscape architect. See Foreword to J. C. Shepherd and Geoffrey Jellicoe *Italian Gardens of the Renaissance* (4th edition 1986): 'John Shepherd advising Elisabeth Scott was to win for her the international competition for the Shakespeare Memorial Theatre ... mainly through sense of landscape and sympathy to site'. In 1970 Jellicoe contributed a plan to the Stratford-upon-Avon Corporation for a re-development of the Bridgefoot area around the new Hilton Hotel, which he based on the fan-shaped concept of Scott's theatre. The original, finalised plans for the theatre, approved by the Borough Surveyor in August 1929, survive in the S.B.T. Records Office BRR49/1/1308.

99. *Evening Standard*, 5 January 1928.
100. *Birmingham Despatch*, 5 January 1928.
101. *Daily Telegraph*, 6 January 1928.
102. *Builder*, 22 April 1932; The *Lady*, 28 April 1932.
103. After completion of the theatre Elisabeth Scott was to work on building expansions at Newnham College, Cambridge, with J. C. Shepherd and John Breakwell. She retired from practice during the Second World War, and died Mrs George Richards on 19 June 1972. *The Times*, 24 June 1972.
104. Brock and Pringle *op.cit.* note p.34.
105. Souvenir of the theatre's opening, 1932. Concrete and Portland stone were favoured building materials for many other important sites constructed in the early 1930s, among them the buildings of Oxford Circus, and Regent Street stores such as Liberty's and Dickens and Jones in London, where designs were from architects such as Norman Shaw and Sir Reginald Blomfield. See *Academy Architecture and Architectural Review*, lx, 1928.

106. *Birmingham Post*, 6 January 1928.
107. *Observer*, 8 January 1928; Brock and Pringle *op.cit.* p.36.
108. Reprinted in *The Festival Review*, xxxvi, 30 April-5 May 1928, pp.6-9; of Gray's 12 main suggestions only the use of the cyclorama and stage lifts were incorporated into Stratford's theatre design. Despite innovative work of Tyrone Guthrie and Tanya Moiseiwitsch in the 1950s and 60s, 'In many respects ... theatre today is only just catching up with Gray's far-sighted vision'; see Richard Cave *Terence Gray and the Cambridge Festival Theatre*, (Cambridge, 1980).
109. Harold Ridge was a close friend of Terence Gray and was able to incorporate Gray's idea of concealed light sources into the Memorial Theatre although the number of lights was far short of Gray's view that they should 'be projected from every point of the compass.' Gray in Cave *op.cit.* Maurice Chesterton also consulted Gray on a variety of technical matters.
110. Detailed brickwork description in *Architectural Review*, June 1932, p.245.
111. Archibald Flower to Harley Granville-Barker, Letter 34, 18 May 1928 of S.C.L. correspondence cited above. Fordham Flower wrote in his obituary to Bridges-Adams in RST Annual Report 1965 that to save costs the fly-tower as constructed was twenty feet lower than Bridges-Adams had originally wanted.
112. Note *Architectural Review*, June 1932 p.223.
113. *Architectural Review*, June 1932. See also R. H. Wilenski *ibid.* and *The Studio* August 1936, pp.79-84.
114. Joy Cass 'The architect's draughtsman.' Manuscript in S.C.L.
115. J. C. Squire in *Architectural Review*, June 1932. For illustration of this ceiling see Jellicoe *op.cit.* pl.10.
116. S.B.T. Records Offiçe BRR2/12/1.
117. *Stratford-upon-Avon Herald* report on Memorial Governors' Meeting in *Theatre Records*, xxiii, p.9, April 1929.
118. Souvenir of 1932 opening of the theatre.
119. Borough Records in S.B.T. Records Office BRR2/12/1.9 October.
120. This plan was never fulfilled. See drawing in *American Architect* 1927, at S.C.L. P.71.2 General/1927.
121. Report of S.M.T. Governors *Theatre Records*, xxiii, March 1930. For B. L. Hurst's report on the foundation problems see S.M.T. Minute Book 2, 21 November 1929.
122. *Architect and Building News*, April 1932, p.114; see Jellicoe *op.cit.* p.43 for details of foundations.
123. *Birmingham Mail*, 2 July 1929. See also note 32 above. The trowel was specially designed and made at Stratford School of Art by F.A.B. Holte and Mabel Scriven. S.M.T. Minute Book 2, p.76. It survives in Freemasons' Hall, Gt. Queen Street, London.
124. Day and Trewin *op.cit.* p.209.
125. *Daily Express*, 3 July 1929.

126. *Stratford-upon-Avon Herald*, 11 April 1930.
127. *Birmingham Mail*, 24 October 1930.
128. *Builder*, 22 April 1932.
129. Archibald Flower to Harley Granville-Barker, Letter 34, 18 May 1928, of correspondence cited above.
130. Ruth Ellis *The Shakespeare Memorial Theatre* (1948) p.67; *Stratford-upon-Avon Herald* reported the Prince's speech and the failure of loudspeakers which meant that the crowd could hear little, although the radio outside broadcast brought the proceedings to homes throughout the nation.
131. *Architectural Review*, June 1932, p.243.
132. *Architect and Building News*, April 1932; Gertrude Hermes (1901-1983) was born in Kent, of German parents. She studied art in Hammersmith, specialising in sculpture and engraving. After creating the pool and the fountain court at the Shakespeare Memorial Theatre she specialised in portraits in bronze, and also engraved illustrations for the Gregynog Press and early Penguin books. See *Dictionary of National Biography 1981-1985*, and *The Times*, obituary 11 May 1983; also biographical notes by her daughter in: Judith Russell *The Wood-Engravings of Gertrude Hermes*. (1993). In 1928 she lived in Hammersmith, close to designer Norman Wilkinson and may, perhaps, have become known to the theatre architects through his connections. See the *Brentford Times*, 29 April 1932.
133. *Architect and Building News*, April 1932; *Architectural Review*, June 1932, p.243 for metalwork detail and p.244 for fountain.
134. *Architectural Review*, June 1932 p.255 illustration of curtains.
135. *Architect and Building News*, April 1932. Walpole Champneys taught design at the Architectural Association. He had remained in touch with former student John C. Shepherd who invited him to join the theatre team.
136. *Architect and Building News*, 22 April 1932; stalls door detailed in Jellicoe *op.cit.* Figure 77.
137. *Architectural Review*, June 1932, illustration of doors pp.252-3.
138. *Architectural Review*, June 1932, p.256.
139. Kemp and Trewin *op.cit.* pp.158 and 164.
140. Royal Box illustrated in *Morning Post*, 22 April 1932.
141. Conditions January 1927. See Brock and Pringle *op.cit.* p.33.
142. Fingerplate details, see Jellicoe *op.cit.* Figure 4; *Architectural Review*, June 1932, p.252.
143. Colour scheme details, see Jellicoe *op.cit.* facing pl.31; in a letter 5 October 1931 to his brother, Archibald, Spenser Flower described making the choice of the specially designed seating that Austin had suggested. S.M.T archive Box 1 S.C.L.
144. Brock and Pringle *op.cit.* p.89 note 47; *Evesham Journal*, 27 February 1932 for biographical details of Polunin.
145. The air-extraction system remained in use until the major air-conditioning overhaul in 1976. Brock and Pringle *op.cit.* note 48; vacuum cleaning

extractors allowed two cleaners to work at the same time, *Architectural Review,* June 1932 p. lxxii; *Birmingham Post,* 20 June 1932.

146. *Birmingham Post,* letter from Homery Folkes, 24 August 1931.
147. *Birmingham Post,* 25 August 1931; The *Lady,* 28 April 1932.
148. Brock and Pringle *op.cit.* p.35.
149. William Bridges-Adams in a letter to *Architects' Journal,* 24 February 1951. See Beauman *op.cit.* p.361 note 6; Brock and Pringle *op.cit.* note 49. Yet it was Bridges-Adams who had insisted on the fixed proscenium arch while the architects, with advice from Terence Gray, were more in favour of a flexible frame to the stage. See Jellicoe *op.cit.* Introduction. Information also from interview with Sir Geoffrey Jellicoe, January 1993.
150. In a letter, 28 September 1931, Spenser Flower described to Archie Flower modifications for the safer operation of the rolling stages that he had arranged with Knight, whom he described as 'a very quiet and experienced man and a real engineer.' S.M.T. archive Box 1 S.C.L.
151. Also *Richard III,* Royal Shakespeare Theatre 1970.
152. It has only been since the late 1980s, towards the end of a season, with five or six large sets in the repertoire, that storage within the tower has created real difficulties.
153. Today the rehearsal room houses the computers of the box office advance and telephone booking departments. In 1932 the stage door was close to the dressing rooms, protected by the canopy under which the gallery patrons queued. This became the administration entrance when the stage door moved in the 1950s to beyond the carpenter's door below the Victorian carriageway arch.
154. Iain Mackintosh *Architect, Actor and Audience* (1993) p.104.
155. Day and Trewin *op.cit.* p.164.
156. Letter to *The Times,* 2 May 1929. In S.M.T. Minute Book 3, 4 March 1933, the final cost of the theatre building was £162,786, to which would be added a projected £11,360 for the Conference Hall. In 1935 the Governors recorded that the theatre was entirely free of debt and all the building work was paid for.
157. For details of the contribution made by the American Shakespeare Foundation see Beauman *op.cit.* pp.128-129, etc.; insurance payment, reported *The Times* 27 May 1926; W. Bridges-Adams, quoted from the *Listener,* xxi, no 535, 13 April 1939, p.794.
158. *Evesham Journal,* 17 January 1931. In Elisabeth Scott's competition entry were designs that envisaged the complete demolition of the walls of the old theatre, to erect a conference hall on the site with a facade that echoed the north entrance of the new theatre. The plans for this survive in the S.B.T. Records Office. BRR49/1/1641.
159. *The Times,* 30 November 1931.
160. *Birmingham Post,* 21 December 1931.
161. *Daily Mail,* 22 November 1932.

162. These curtains were not completed until March 1935. See the receipted invoice from Frank Organ, 61-62 Henley Street, Stratford-upon-Avon for eight pairs of curtains £6 1s 0d in invoice book in S.C.L.
163. *Morning Post,* 17 April 1933. The final layout for the gardens did not follow Elisabeth Scott's designs as new plans were prepared by the Corporation's own advisers. The river navigation beyond the canal basin was not re-opened until 1973.
164. S.M.T. Minute Book 11; Michael Kimberley *op.cit.* p.38.
165. In 1970 a report on the layout of the Bancroft gardens and the Bridgefoot area was commissioned from the landscape architect Sir Geoffrey Jellicoe, but his designs were never fully implemented; see note 98 above and Michael Spens *Gardens of the Mind. The Genius of Geoffrey Jellicoe* (1990).
166. S.M.T. Minute Book 11, 30 September 1955 and October 1956; see note 88 above.
167. The plans and an architect's sketch for the 1938 extensions were approved by the Borough Surveyor's office in December 1936. See S.B.T. Records Office BRR49/1/2281. Elisabeth Scott's new firm was based at 12 York Buildings, Adelphi, London WC1 and later moved to Pond House, Stoke Row, near Henley on Thames.
168. S.M.T. Minute Book 3, 20 March 1937. The cellulin did not wear well and repairs had to be carried out within a year. S.M.T. archive Box 1, S.C.L.
169. *Architect and Building News,* cliii, 25 March 1938, pp.356-359; see *Stratford-upon-Avon Herald,* 11 December 1936.
170. R.S.T. Minute Book 4, December 1966.
171. There had been a proposal in 1934 for 90 extra seats in the gallery, S.M.T. Minute Book 3, 22 November 1934. The 1936 alterations affected the air circulation and later extra fans had to be added above the rear of the balcony, and further ventilation extractor fans were placed at the back of the stalls in 1955: S.M.T. Minute Book 11, 21 March 1955. Scott, Chesterton and Shepherd designed the gallery refreshment room, above the main restaurant, which was created at the same time as the alterations to the gallery seating in 1935-6; For plans see S.B.T. Records Office BRR49/1/2068; S.M.T. Minute Book 3, 3 December 1936.
172. Brock and Pringle *op.cit.* p.81; *Daily Telegraph,* 27 September 1943; acoustics expert, Hope Bagenal, had suggested adding a felt pelmet over the forestage, but this was not implemented, S.M.T. Minute Book 3, 17 February 1934.
173. Richard Leacroft *Theatre and Playhouse* (1984).
174. *Birmingham Post,* 31 January 1944.
175. S.M.T. Minute Book 3, 1 October 1946.
176. Anthony Quayle *A Time to Speak* (1990) p.322.
177. Lutyens had worked on plans for a National Theatre site opposite the Victoria and Albert Museum in Kensington, where an Islamic centre now stands. The next site chosen was between County Hall and Charing Cross

bridge, for which O'Rorke designed an opera house and a theatre. The National Theatre plans were redrawn by O'Rorke when the site was changed to the South Bank alongside the Festival Hall, where the Hayward Gallery was eventually built. O'Rorke's plans were never completed, although a foundation stone was laid in 1951. Government ideas on funding changed and the National Theatre, built to the east of Waterloo Bridge, was eventually designed by Sir Denys Lasdun and opened in 1977. See *The Times,* O'Rorke obituary 1972; Iain Mackintosh. 'Scene individual or poem unlimited.' In *Architectural Review,* clxi, 959. January 1977.

178. These are 1954 figures.

179. Soon after the opening of the 1951 season all the seat backs had to be replaced by the installers, the long established architectural and ecclesiastical metal work firm H. H. Martyns of Cheltenham, as already a number were breaking, showing their design and materials were unsuited to heavy, continual use; S.M.T. Minute Book 3, 21 April 1951.

180. Tibor Reich had been born in Budapest in 1918 and came to England after studying in Vienna. He was in the Textile Department at Leeds University for five years before setting up his firm at Clifford Chambers, near Stratford-upon-Avon in 1946. Later commissions carried out by 'Tibor', as the firm was professionally known, were the interior fabrics for the liner Queen Elizabeth II, for Concorde airliners and for the Shakespeare Centre built at Stratford-upon-Avon in 1964. Details of colour schemes for the theatre are from an unidentified journal article supplied by Tibor Reich.

181. *Leamington Spa Courier,* 26 January 1951.

182. *Sunday Times,* 1 July 1951; the architect's drawings and steelwork plans for the 1951 alterations are in the S.B.T. Records Office at BRR49/1/3695. They were approved by the planning authority on 2 October 1950.

183. S.M.T. Minute Book 3, 28 September 1950, contains an itemised estimate for the alterations. Dressing rooms 9-12 were re-numbered in 1993 to become 12, 12a, 14 and 15.

184. Details of the foyer alterations supplied in interview with Bob Harvey, 1992. Henry Hope and Sons had previously been involved with the theatre as advisers to Elisabeth Scott on window engineering in 1930. In 1947 the front seats of the gallery had become bookable in advance and were renamed the balcony. Gallery queuing for unreserved seats was finally abolished in 1948. S.M.T. Minute Book 3, 8 January 1947. Seat prices in 1947 were: stalls and circle: 10s 6d, 8s, 6s, 4s; balcony reserved: 2s 6d and gallery unreserved: 1s 6d. 1948-1950 prices were stalls and circle: 10s 6d, 7s 6d, 5s and all the balcony was 2s 6d. After the 1951 alterations: stalls and circle: 12s 6d, 9s 6d, 6s; balcony: 4s, 2s 6d; standing: 2s 6d.

185. *Coventry Evening Telegraph,* 15 November 1958.

186. S.M.T. Minute Book 4, 21 April 1961; and Iain Mackintosh in *Architectural Review* clxi, p.959, January 1977. A copy of Sean Kenny's 1961 plan, in association with Ove Arup and Partners, for the complete re-construction of

the theatre's interior survives in S.C.L.

187. The alterations also included the loss of the Polunin safety curtain which had become very dilapidated. It was painted over in black.

188. R.S.C. Minute Book 11; David Addenbrooke *The Royal Shakespeare Company. The Peter Hall Years* (1973) p.44. The proscenium arch has remained 29 feet 9 inches wide although the height was increased to 21 feet in 1957, and is now 23 feet 9 inches from the stage floor.

189. Vickers press release, 1972. The architect, Bob Harvey, was aware of potential sight-line problems with suggestions for alterations to the auditorium. For the side-balcony changes in 1972 he proposed the cantilever solution to prevent a need for support from below envisaged by Christopher Morley.

190. Major contributions to the Centenary fund included the Shakespeare Birthplace Trust (£10,000) and the American Friends of the R.S.C. ($10,000).

191. The basic rake in the 1970s was 1 in 8. See unpublished notes by Roger Howells on stage changes each year, in S.C.L.

192. These were experiments that sought to ignore the restrictions of the proscenium but, as theatre designer and historian, Iain Mackintosh, said in *Architect, Actor and Audience,* (1993) p.95:

> *There is a limit to flexibility in the proscenium zone; you cannot change a theatre such as the Royal Shakespeare ... into a thrust stage by adding a few rows at each side of the stage where select members of the audience sit uneasily on benches like reluctant ice hockey players.*

193. All these changes were achieved without the need to close the restaurants by installing the new windows on the outside before removing the existing units within.

194. James Keteltas Hackett (1869-1926), the son of the actor James H. Hackett (1800-1871), had acted at Stratford in the season of 1922. He died a few months after the fire that destroyed the first Memorial Theatre and his bequest was of substantial help to the re-building fund. When Hackett's Memorial Trust was wound up over £18,600 was paid into the theatre's funds. R.S.T. Minute Book 11, 5 June 1961 and 19 September 1963. Another plaque by the fountain now records the names of donors to the 1975 appeal and centenary garden. A nearby case has displayed the Pragnell Award silver bowl since its inception in 1990 as an annual award to recognise significant contributions to the understanding or appreciation of William Shakespeare.

195. After war service Paul Morgan worked again at the library for a few months before pursuing his career that led him to become a senior member of the Bodleian Library staff.

196. S.M.T. Minute Book 11, 30 September 1955.

197. The shelves were first installed at Avonside, Mill Lane, where Vaughan traded from home in accommodation rented from the theatre; later the units were moved to his shop premises in Chapel Street.
198. S.M.T. Minute Book 3, 13 October 1953.
199. *Birmingham Express,* 21 April 1904; *Henry V,* Act 4, scene 3.
200. *The Times,* 2 May 1905; *Birmingham Weekly Mercury,* 6 May 1905.
201. The Stratford-upon-Avon Guild had been set up at 20 Henley Street, after the First World War, with financial assistance from the Flower family, to provide skilled opportunities for wounded war veterans in 'architectural decoration, plasterwork, leadwork, carving, mural painting and stained glass'. See *The Gala Book,* 1927. For details of the 1925 ceremonies see *Stratford-upon-Avon Herald,* 26 June 1925.
202. *Birmingham Post,* 24 April 1950.
203. S.M.T. Annual Report 1939; this was the site finally replaced in 1991 by the new purpose-built workshops on the Timothy's Bridge Road industrial estate.
204. 'House of Commons Evacuation and Emergency Papers, 1939-41'. HLRO 313/23; *In Parliament,* 1939-50 (House of Commons Library Document 2) (1991) pp.5-7.
205. S.M.T. Minute Book 3, 9 September 1948.
206. Edward Carrick was the son of Edward Gordon Craig and thus grandson of Ellen Terry, who had appeared as Katharine of Aragon at the S.M.T. in 1902 on the day the theatre appointed her a Life Governor. Carrick was in Stratford in 1949 to design the production of *Macbeth.*
207. Report in S.M.T. Minute Book 3, 28 September 1949; See also S.M.T. Minute Book 3, 16 November 1949, 25 March 1950.
208. J. R. Mulryne and Margaret Shewring *This Golden Round* (Stratford-upon-Avon, 1989).
209. *ibid* pp.10 and 12.
210. Interview with Michael Reardon, 1992. For an illustration of the Sabbioneta theatre see Marvin Carlson *Places of Performance* (Ithaca, N.Y., 1989) p.168. For plans and comments on the Sabbioneta theatre (1588) and Teatro Farnese (1618) see Jellicoe *op.cit.* pp.17-18; there is also a useful description of the Sabbioneta theatre in the introduction to Stephen Joseph, ed. *Actor and Architect* (Manchester, 1964), pp.3-4.
211. *Coventry Evening Telegraph,* 1 November and 1 December 1978; *Stage and Television Today,* 14 December 1978.
212. The final cost of the scheme was not fully disclosed but Koch is believed to have donated between £1,800,000 and £2 million. See *Daily Telegraph,* 14 November 1986.
213. The dormer windows are on the angles of the roof instead of in the facets as Unsworth had placed them.
214. The Royal Fine Arts Commission objected to the loss of the carriageway arch but the local planning authority decided to ignore the objection.

215. *RSC News,* Winter 1984; the swan design and its encircling lettering had been completed by Cambridge typographer, Will Carter. This design was based on an idea of Villard de Honnecourt, an early thirteenth-century French architect and draughtsman, whose drawings survive in the Bibliothèque Nationale in Paris. *Daily Telegraph,* 21 and 28 November 1960, see E. H. Gombrich *Art and Illusion* (1960) p.173, figure 143.
216. *Stage and Television Today,* 11 April 1986.
217. Michael Reardon in *Daily Telegraph,* 28 April 1986.
218. Mulryne and Shewring *op.cit.* p.11.
219. *Forte.* Winter issue, 1986.
220. Margaret Ingram in *Stratford-upon-Avon Herald,* 2 May 1986.
221. Interview with Michael Reardon, 1992.
222. Anne Fitzgerald *Stage and Television Today,* 11 April 1986.
223. S.M.T. Minute Book 3, 20 June 1946 records the removal of the ivy.
224. R.S.T. Minute Book 4, 21 April 1961.
225. R.S.T. Minute Book 4, 25 September 1963.
226. S.M.T. Minute Book 11, 16 July 1954.
227. R.S.T. Minute Book 11, 16 June 1963. Consideration of the workshop move was deferred in July 1963 and abandoned the following year.
228. See Addenbrooke *op.cit.* p.52-53.
229. Sean Kenny 'The shape of the theatre', Fig 7, in Stephen Joseph, ed. *op.cit.* p.61.
230. R.S.T. Minute Book 11, *Finance Committee,* 24 May 1964.
231. See Beauman *op.cit.* p.297.
232. *ibid.* p.311.
233. *ibid.* p.320; Goodbody also worked in 1972 on productions at the Aldwych Theatre.
234. The Goodbody report spoke firstly of internal work which might become suitable for public performance, and secondly of the aim to provide a second auditorium for a potentially local audience of traditionally non-theatre going sections of society, for school pupils and students at local educational establishments, and for visitors who did not wish to see the plays of Shakespeare in the main theatre. She went on to outline the kind of work she envisaged being presented, most of which did in fact happen in the next few years. Trevor Nunn's memorandum to the company on 22 January 1974 stated: 'Work in The Other Place will be geared towards sections of the community who, for various reasons, are not regular members of our audience.'
235. The planning permission granted for The Other Place in April 1973 had included the condition that the Company must 'ensure the development does not become permanently established in the absence of a comprehensive and well-planned scheme for the site.'
236- Ian Herbert 'Stratford's Third Theatre', in *Sightline* xxv, 4, November
239. 1991. p.p.18-23.

Select Bibliography

Much of the research for this work is drawn directly from the archives of the Shakespeare Memorial Theatre and the Royal Shakespeare Company, deposited at the Shakespeare Centre Library, Stratford-upon-Avon, including Annual Reports, *Theatre Records* (of newscuttings 1875-1992), and the photographic collections of the theatre and of the Shakespeare Birthplace Trust Records Office.

Secondary material consulted includes:

David Addenbrooke *The Royal Shakespeare Company. The Peter Hall Years* (1973).

Architect and Building News, April 1932; also 23 March 1938.

Architectural Review, June 1932.

Robert Bearman *Stratford-upon-Avon. A History of its Streets and Buildings* (1988).

Sally Beauman *The Royal Shakespeare Company. A History of Ten Decades* (Oxford, 1982).

John Bott *The Figure of the House. An Illustrated Record of the Building of Stratford's Theatre* (Stratford-upon-Avon, 1974).

Susan Brock and Marian J. Pringle *The Shakespeare Memorial Theatre 1919-1945* (Cambridge, 1984).

Marvin Carlson *Places of Performance* (Ithaca, N.Y., 1989).

Richard Cave *Terence Gray and the Cambridge Festival Theatre* (Cambridge, 1980).

M. C. Day and J. C. Trewin *The Shakespeare Memorial Theatre* (1932).

Christian Deelman *The Great Shakespeare Jubilee* (1964).

Ruth Ellis *The Shakespeare Memorial Theatre* (1948).

Charles Edward Flower *A History of the Shakespeare Memorial* (Stratford-upon-Avon, 2nd. ed. 1882).

Sarah Flower *Great Aunt Sarah's Diary, 1846-1892* (priv. print., 1964).

Richard Foulkes *The Shakespeare Tercentenary of 1864* (1984).

E. H. Gombrich *Art and Illusion* (1960).

A. Stuart Gray *Edwardian Architecture* (1985).

Tyrone Guthrie, Richard Southern, and others *Actor and Architect,* edited by Stephen Joseph (Manchester, 1964).

Ian Herbert 'Stratford's Third Theatre', in *Sightline* xxv, 4, November 1991.

Geoffrey A. Jellicoe *The Shakespeare Memorial Theatre* (1933).

T. C. Kemp and J. C. Trewin *The Stratford Festival. A History of the Shakespeare Memorial Theatre* (Birmingham, 1953).

Michael Kimberley *Lord Ronald Gower's Monument to Shakespeare* (Stratford-upon-Avon, 1989).

Richard Leacroft *Theatre and Playhouse* (1984).

Iain Mackintosh 'Scene individual or poem unlimited', in *Architectural Review,* cxli, no.959, January 1977.

------------ -------------- *Architecture, Actor and Audience* (1993).

Paul Morgan 'The Shakespeare Memorial Theatre and Freemasonry' in *Warwickshire Masonic Record,* ix, October 1985.

J. R. Mulryne and Margaret Shewring *This Golden Round* (Stratford-upon-Avon, 1989).

Anthony Quayle *A Time to Speak* (1990).

Edwin O. Sachs *Modern Opera Houses and Theatres* (1897).

James Sargant 'Five Weeks and Two Days.' in *Sightline,* xvii, 2, Autumn 1983.

Philip Styles 'The Borough of Stratford-upon-Avon and Alveston', in *Victoria County History of Warwickshire,* iii (1945).

Index

H

I

J

K

L